KATABATIC WIND

GOOD CRAIC FUELED BY FUMES FROM THE ABYSS

BY STEPHEN CRIMI

LOGOSOPHIA

KATABATIC WIND
GOOD CRAIC FUELED BY FUMES FROM THE ABYSS
BY STEPHEN CRIMI

LOGOSOPHIA

Logosophia, LLC

Logosophia, LLC
90 Oteen Church Road
Asheville, NC 28805
www.logosophiabooks.com
logosophiabooks@gmail.com

"Hamlet and Arjuna Handle Crisis" is fully reworked from the much shorter "The Outcome of Crisis in *Hamlet* and the *Bhagavad Gītā*" originally published in *Moksha Journal*, Vol 3 No. 2, 1986. "The Sacred Origins of Western Civilization" was originally published in *Journal for Anthroposophy in Australia*, Issue No. 4, Summer-December 2011.

Library of Congress-in-Publication Data
Crimi, Stephen
Katabatic Wind: Good Craic Fueled by Fumes from the Abyss

ISBN 978-0-9966394-1-5
Distributed by Small Press Distribution
Non-Fiction
Cover design and layout by Susan Yost
Cover art: Diana fresco from the Villa of Ariadne, Stabiae, National Archaeological Museum, Naples.

for Krys: my love, my lodestar, my light…

Details of a Second Occultation

Betty Roszak

I was born in a mask
under the sign of contradiction.
Yet the fountains shone in my mind.
In order to live I had to die
in that consuming fire,
torn apart, a body of broken bones.
I had to leave the unquiet city
of this world, emptied by death,
beyond all horizons,
in no direction and all directions.
Back to the very beginning
to find what was there all along.
Beyond everything into darkness,
the deepest darkest void.
Darkness below, above and all around.

Everything dwindles.
The angel whispers: "Choose!"
Everything else is taken away.
Only the whisper and the choice.
A cloud surrounds, a darkness covers
an anguish of helpless desire.
Death is the entrance
and the heart turns to stone.

The first taste is utterly new
and completely familiar.
A door opens and I fall
through immense depths.
Emptiness empties me,
and I am more myself
than ever before.

The mask falls away
not in a sudden flash
but imperceptibly, gradually
in shadows and silence and night.
Images vanish. I see nothing,
hear nothing, feel nothing.
What was hidden was so near
it's inside and outside
and everywhere.

I've travelled to a far region,
yet secretly I've been here all the time.
There never was an abyss.
I do not fall into anything,
there is no space, or there is all space.
The next step is not a step.

It is infinitely still. Words fall apart.
There are no more names, no forms.
This is not what I'm talking about.
It is only the beginning.
I have just begun to exist.
I don't know who I am, everything
turned inside out. Nobody realizes it
but the beats of my blood.
Nobody realizes it
but the whole earth.

TABLE OF CONTENTS

Introduction

The katabatic wind blown here flows bidirectionally. Meteorologically speaking, it whistles down from mountains or arctic ice sheets, from high to low, journeying from inaccessible places to the agora, the roiling marketplace. Traditionally, the mountains are from whence wisdom is found and dispensed, the homes of the gods, a place we look up to for aspiration and inspiration.

Yet there is another *katabasis*, from the Ancient Greek, meaning 'to go down', to travel from this world to the underworld. There, the chthonic gods and goddesses are just as real, just as powerful, and maybe just a little edgy for being neglected for so long. They were accustomed to an occasional visit: Odysseus, Orpheus, Inanna, Pythagoras, Parmenides, Aeneas, and the Christ—as well as all the unremembered healer-prophet-priests called *iatromantis*—all perform a *katabasis*. It is the journey of the initiate, to die before you die, thence to live twice-born: once of the flesh, and again of wisdom, *sophia*.

Imaginally, this katabatic wind blows *up* from these realms, a wisdom carried back within those able to hold to it. Or sometimes it just seeps up through the cracks in our being, like the Pythian oracle priestess altered from the subterranean fumes. Often we sense something significant has infiltrated our mundane routine, but its meaning fades like a dissipating dream.

There is a third usage for *katabasis* in the ancient texts, a military retreat or maneuver from the inland to the coast, with an *anabasis* describing a movement in the opposite direction. *Katabasis* connecting to both the military and initiation has a poignant irony. One of the great losses for western culture is any form of real initiation. What remains of the coming-of-age rites in the Abrahamic religions is anemic. There are a number of people, influenced by indigenous cultures, trying to bring potency back to some sort of initiation. But as helpful as those traditional waters are to individuals, as a culture, the West has lost all connection to the sacred spring it arose from. Sadly, there is never salvation from without. And since the initiatory need has to get filled in some way, it gets supplanted by the military. The longing so many young people feel for meaning becomes projected onto a fraudulent gladiatorial romantic ideal. Then they receive for their trouble an *anti-initiation*, that is, an investiture not of wisdom and purposeful life, but of violence and meaningless death. We don't need long sermons on where that has taken us as a civilization.

The kernel of these essays—with the original meaning of 'attempts'—is loss, longing for return, and the grief of living in a society without even an inkling of its sacred origin story. The masterpiece of Persian poetry, Jalal-uddin Rumi's massive *Mathnavi*, begins by showing how all art stems from loss. A reed is cut from a stream bed, and immediately sings of its longing to return home. All true art—sacred art, sublime art—attempts to resonate with our numinous origin. All other art, as James Joyce said, is pornography: either enticement or revulsion.

There is no pretense of purpose in publishing this book. At best, one hopes for a homeopathic dosage dropped in the global flood of ignorance disseminated from the West. Longing for transcendence crosses the spectrum these days, from New Age ascensionists to Christian rapture-seekers. But in spite of passing the winter 2012 'end date', the Kali Yuga supposedly being over, and the ever-impending quantum jump in consciousness, everything looks the same from here. Even jihadism and S&M are bizarre mutations of the desire to outstrip quotidian existence. Humans will endure and/or cause any suffering to avoid facing themselves. We are always looking outside for salvation. If anything, these essays are a call to look for our sounding note within.

The hope then, is that a *katabatic wind* carries you to the dark, silent depths of your being, where the origin note trilling the sacred song at the core of creation rents your heart, filling your longing with wisdom, incarnating that melody to illumine life itself.

"Lux in Tenebris" by Evelyn De Morgan, 1895.

These essays have been thoroughly rewritten from various writings composed mostly during the past decade. Some were previously published, and some flatly rejected by various journals. As anyone who has been in the construction business knows, it is far easier to raze a building and start from the ground than to try to keep the structure and refurbish. There will be hidden cracks and leaks, rooms that need repurposing, new color schemes, and the overwhelming fear that the whole thing will just fall apart.

There are three sections of writings. Breakfast, the most important meal of the day, consists of five pieces drawn from the Greek and Indian traditions. The first explores the origins of the Orpheus-Eurydice myth, and the second looks at a particular *Ṛgvedic* chant in terms of death, ancient and modern. It came from a class I gave in Asheville on Sanskrit and the *Ṛgvedic* vision. The third and longest is a completely reworked piece juxtaposing the stories of Hamlet and Arjuna. The original was about a quarter as long, and published in *Mokṣha Journal*. The fourth piece comes from what we'll call a download in meditation, of a breathing practice designed to balance the tendency for yoga practitioners to desire transcendence into out-of-body states while ignorant of the ground they stand upon. It is possible that yoga as practiced today in this country is completely unhinged from its original vision, and hopefully aspects of these writings will point anyone interested back toward remembrance.

The translation of the *Puruṣa Sukta* poem took so very long, it did me the favor of cementing the realization that Vedic translation is not my wheelhouse, and best left to those of superior declension.

There is a saying within permaculture circles, "There's a lot of work to do, but if it's not fun, we're not going to do it!" Lunch is lighter fare than breakfast, starting with three short exegeses, two of 'popular' songs, and a look at the mystic number 108. Next is a piece on the sacred geometry of baseball, overwhelmingly the most esoteric of games. No baseball journal would touch it.

Supper's 'retroduction' recapitulates the main themes of losing and remembering our connection to the sacred origins of culture. The first piece describes an ayahuasca ritual, assigning sobriquets, of course. Ultimately, there is a talk given at the Rudolf Steiner House in Sydney in 2011. It has been lightly edited for clarity, and was originally published in *Journal for Anthroposophy in Australia*. It humbly attempts to present a complete broad overview of western sacred origins and the rails subsequent thought ran away upon.

The Irish love nothing better than what they call 'good craic': enjoyable and uplifting conversation. What better discourse could prevail than amongst our higher selves?

Asheville, NC
Winter Solstice, 2015

I. Greco-Indian Peregrination

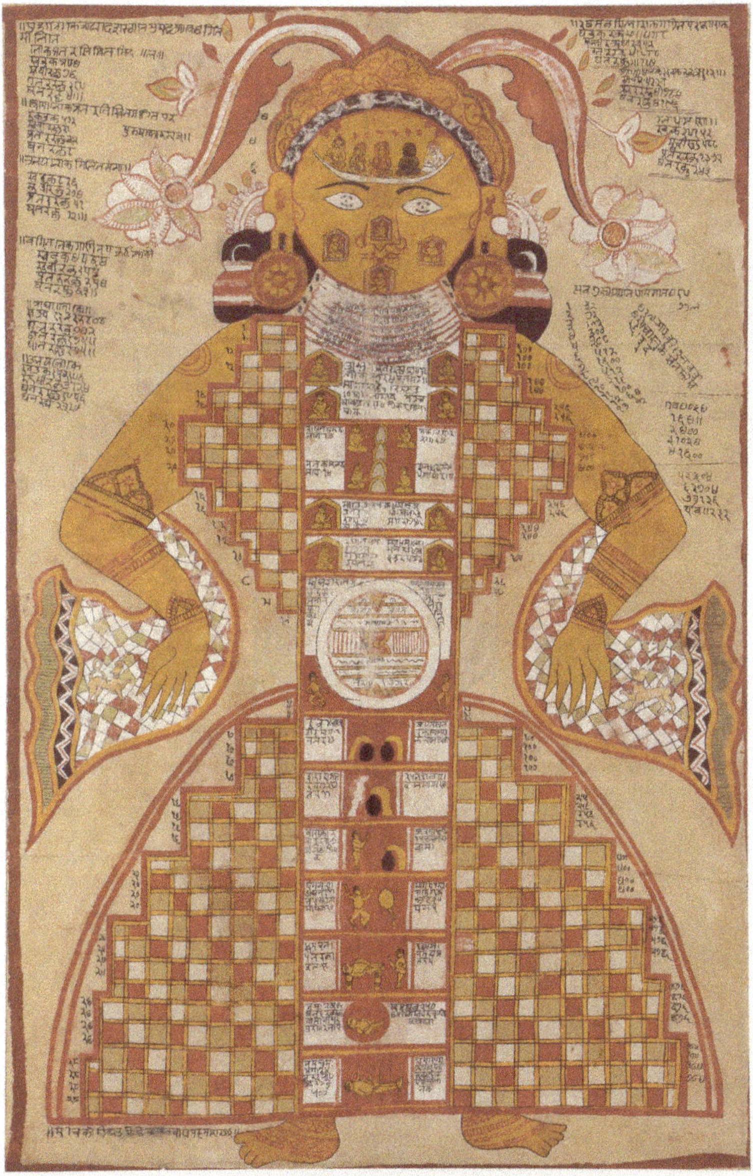

Yantra painting 1700's, Museo Nacional de Anthropologia, Madrid.

Listen, O dearly beloved!
I am the reality of the world, the center of the circumference,
I am the parts and the whole.
I am the will established between Heaven and Earth,
I have created perception in you in order
to be the object of my perception.

If then you perceive me, you perceive yourself.
But you cannot perceive me through yourself.
It is only through my eyes that you see me and see yourself,
Through your eyes you cannot see me.

– Ibn Arabi, "Sophianic Poem"

Invisible hive, has it no small door
we could find if we stood
quite still and listened?

– Denise Levertov, "Dream 'Cello"

Myth Shift

Imagine Orpheus in actuality rescuing Eurydice from the underworld, instead of watching her despairingly re-ferried to the dismal shades of Hades as he reaches vainly for her outstretched hands. Imagine he navigates all the netherworld obstacles and traps, then pleases the deities ruling there with his extemporaneous poetry and singing, and surfaces with his true love, revivified: Eurydice in the flesh.

According to scraps of mytho-archaeological evidence found referring to the Orpheus and Eurydice story, this successful return was likely the original outcome. What happened for such a reversal of a foundational Greek myth to occur? We only know that it did, and here imagine that the revision followed a watershed shift in that culture's relationship to the divine feminine.

When spying back on the Greek world, Classical scholarship tends to read ancient life from the perspective of the contemporary brain, though luckily this is changing more and more. Scholars often interpret the past through one of the reigning myths of our time, that of Progress. The Myth of Progress, born of the industrial age and its materialist paradigm, has us moving toward an ideal of greater faster more and better. And because indeed there have been, say, first steam trains then bullet trains; jalopies then Lamborghini's; bi-planes and then space travel; computers the size of gymnasiums to nano processors on watches; and apparent political shifts in form from authoritarian kingship to authoritarian corporatocracy, we have projected that image onto our human culture. We think that humanity's quality of living has had some sort of concurrent improvement that we call an evolution, and that we know more and better about our ancient fore-bearers than they knew about themselves. The Greeks, of course, would have called this *hubris*.

The current model of rationalist scientism classifies ancient myths as either aggrandized tales of historical personages (a method also favored by many ufologists, with technologically-advanced aliens looked upon as deities), an approach called euhemerism, or depicts these stories as grown from awestruck simple human imaginations, allegorizing normal phenomena like thunder and rainbows into tales of celestial beings. Some later Greeks might actually agree, but earlier Greeks would call it *hubris*.

Either the scientists are right, and not only myths but all human experiences of the divine are but another epiphenomenon of billions of cerebral neurons spurting chemicals across cranial synapses, somehow generating consciousness, and our ability to experience life is a freakish cosmic accident, or just maybe the truth is even weirder. Maybe the gods are real.

If the gods are in some way alive now—forgotten yet pertinent—this apparent physical world is actually a dumb artifact of its divine origins, a limited sensory and temporal experience constricted from what we once knew as immortal omniscients. Then mythological realms in fact pertain to *us*, and are germane in risking a descent to recover the remembrance of who we really are. Or maybe that is *hubris*.

What shifted in the ancient world so that the myths informing classic Greek culture morphed? There is a preponderance of evidence, though not conclusive, that the earliest myths of Orpheus and Eurydice have him successfully returning with her from Hades. The later myth, concretized mainly though the Roman versions of Ovid and Virgil, famously depicts Orpheus losing his beloved just at the moment he thinks he has successfully returned Eurydice from Hades. Such a complete reversal of outcomes would have an enormous effect on the cultural imagination.

The earliest known mention of Orpheus' journey to the underworld appears in Euripides' *Alcestis* (438 BC) where the heroine of the title chooses to die in place of her husband Admetus. While Thanatos—Death himself—awaits, tapping his hourglass watch, Admetus claims he would descend to Hades, entice Pluto and Persephone, and bring her back to the light, if only he had the eloquence of Orpheus. Thus it would seem there is an extant tradition the audience fully recognizes of Orpheus eloquently convincing the Queen and King of the Underworld to return someone who has passed to the shades. Objections abound, claiming that there is some ambiguity, that Admetus never directly mentions Orpheus' underworld journey, but it would be an irrelevant reference if there wasn't already an existing tradition of such a trip. Isocrates (436-338 BC) makes mention of Orpheus "who used to lead the dead from Hades," without mentioning anyone he brings back specifically. Palaephatus (late fourth century BC), who otherwise rationalizes Orpheus' *katabasis*—the Greek word for journeying to the underworld—as merely a long topside walkabout, makes the first mention of Eurydice ('she who gives justice far and wide'—a title more apt for a queen than a maiden) by name, and indicates that she is brought back to this realm alive. The fullest version of a successful return story comes from the Hermesianax of Alexandria (born 340 BC), who names Agriope ('she of the wild face') as the wife returning with Orpheus.

The details are mostly missing, but it looks pretty certain that there was a commonly held myth in the Greek world of a successful return of Eurydice from the underworld by an Orpheus possessing shamanic qualities. Likely there were many stories in circulation. Before addressing the 'twice lost Eurydice' myth it became, there are two anomalies to consider: the Attic relief and Plato's mention of Orpheus in his *Symposium*.

The original of this relief adorned the Altar of Pity in Athens, dating roughly from the time of the Euripides play just mentioned, and depicts from left, Hermes, Eurydice and Orpheus. It is really hard to read what aspect of the story they enact. Hermes, psychopomp and escorter of souls to Hades, is not mentioned in any of the stories that come to us. Clearly he has a tight grip on Eurydice's right arm, and for some reason he is hitching his toga with his right. He looks to have wings on his back, whereas he usually has them on his shoes as befits the swift messenger of the gods. The relief shows an achingly tender moment, probably right after Eurydice's death, of a sad farewell. Her right foot is turned to leave, arm resting on Orpheus' shoulder; while his lyre droops in his left hand, he gently pulls back her veil for a last look. He wears the cap of an initiate. If this shows, as many scholars attest, the second loss of Eurydice at the moment when Orpheus turns to look at her a moment too soon, it has none of the desperate hysteria which that would engender. More likely this Orpheus is already thinking about taking the ultimate journey to retrieve his love.

Hermes, Eurydice and Orpheus, 5th century BC.

Then there is Plato, whose shadow drapes over all we try to know of ancient Greece. In his great dialogue to love, the *Symposium*, his character Phaedrus says, almost in an aside—a place where Plato often veils what is most important to him—that the gods were dismissive of Orpheus' method of retrieving Eurydice. First off, his love is not great enough that he would have died for her (how this could have even been possible is never said), and he was a 'mere minstrel', a 'lukewarm lover', 'lacking courage' to die, who simply schemes his way, *living*, into Hades. Simply? Thus the gods fooled Orpheus, only showing him a phantom, a false shadow of Eurydice, and sent him packing empty-handed. And then they doomed him to die at the hands of women, clearly an ignominious end in Plato's thinking. Plato may have proposed a partial equal education system for both sexes in the *Republic*, but there is no end to his quotable low opinions of women.

The real put-down by Plato here is not the fact that Orpheus is a musician or a poet, whose ilk are banned from his *Republic*, but that he is part of a tradition of shamans who use a type of trickery to cheat death to enter Hades, a tradition embodied in philosophers a generation or two before him, like Pythagoras, Empedocles and Parmenides. They made the *katabasis* to Hades to return not only with a living soul, but also with living wisdom direct from the goddess there. Not to downgrade the person for whom all subsequent philosophy is considered a footnote, but Plato rejected this tradition of going to the underworld for wisdom. Instead his ideals or forms of ultimate knowledge exist—well where? He never quite says. But certainly they are abstracted 'above' and beyond this realm, and they definitely are not in in the underground caves where the mystics just before his time went for knowledge. Instead, in the *Republic*, he specifically depicts the cave as a realm of bondage and ignorance for a reason, and that reason is to transform and bury the shamanic traditions underpinning his culture into the rationalism we celebrate as uniquely Greek today, ignorant of its true origin. Dark, mysterious underground caves are the territory of the divine feminine, while the emerging influence of transcendent ideas broadcast by writers like Plato belong to the masculine world.

"Orpheus and Eurydice" by Gaetano Gandolfi, 18th century.

The versions of Orpheus and Eurydice told through Virgil and Ovid are the only ones that our current culture remembers and transforms into further literature, opera and film. Orpheus is the ur-singer-songwriter, a Thracian, able to charm and heal all creatures through his singing and playing of the lyre. This lyre is the gift of Apollo, who had obtained it from its inventor, Hermes. Orpheus makes stones and trees dance. Having the muse of music, Calliope, as a mother certainly helped.

He falls in love with Eurydice, who may have been an oak nymph and daughter of Apollo. Oak groves were places of knowledge and prophesy for the Greeks as well as the Druids. She falls for him. As everyone gathers for their wedding, she is fatally bitten by a poisonous snake on the heel while running from an attempted rape by Aristaeus, and her shade goes to Hades. Orpheus is more than distraught, and plays so mournfully that the entire cosmos weeps.

Orpheus is advised to make a journey to the land of the dead. Odysseus made this passage, as did Inanna, Pythagoras, Aeneas, and Parmenides. Even Jesus completed the 'Harrowing of Hell'. This hooks in a very real way to the fundamental 'dying before you die' of all traditional sacred initiations. It is not an easy journey, but Orpheus completes it, and when faced with the King and Queen of the Underworld, Pluto and Persephone, he wins them over with his lyre-playing and singing. In this version accepted today, they agree to allow her soul to return, on the condition that he not look behind at her. He obeys, making the difficult ascent, and does turn around in joy, supposedly just as he emerges into above ground light; but Eurydice isn't quite there with him yet, and she fades back into the abyss, arms reaching out in agony. There has always been something very unsatisfactory about this ending.

Then there's the miserable aftermath. Because Orpheus spurns love itself from then on, a group of maenads—frenzied women followers of Bacchus—rip him apart during a Bacchic orgy, with his head and lyre still prophesying as they float down the river Hebrus. There's some connection here with Orpheus supposedly later shifting his priesthood and worship from Bacchus to Apollo. Bacchus-Dionysus was also ripped apart, by the nasty Titans, who were then smote by Zeus, and from this mix of divine and evil ashes humans were born.

"Thracian Girl Carrying the Head of Orpheus on His Lyre"
by Gustav Moreau, 1865.

So what are we to make of this twisted, sadistic outcome? Orpheus offends no gods, breaks no rules. He uses his gift of song for the benefit of all. Eternally punished for turning his head a nanosecond too soon? Even for the Greeks this feels a bit overwrought. The other well-known tormentees—Sisyphus, Prometheus, Tantalus—either pissed off a deity or displayed extreme hubris. In whose vested interest are Eurydice and Orpheus kept apart?

Orpheus is a bridge between the wandering shamans from central Asia and the development of a sacred western mystery tradition in Ancient Greece, Sicily and southern Italy, which spread from the Black Sea to Spain. These itinerant mystics criss-crossed the western ancient world, carrying their god, Hyperborean Apollo, inside them. Traveling in the underworld, meeting and working with deities, and returning with healings, clearings, laws and insights for the community is a core shamanic task.

One way to look at Orpheus' *katabasis* is in terms of the sacred marriage or *hieros gamos*. All *katabasis* is initiatory. All initiation is about connecting with your real self, and in this myth it is the retrieval of his lost feminine self. And it always consists of a death and rebirth. The shamanic underpinnings of Greek—and subsequently our—culture were at stake. A kind of integration of the chthonic and imaginative worlds was a real possibility. Imagine the original version of the myth, where Orpheus and Eurydice emerge together in joy, as a story of reconnection, a resanctification, the sacred masculine and feminine in alchemical union, singing hymns that re-enchant the cosmos as sacred being, over and over.

Something happened in Greece, then Rome, then everywhere in the west. The masculine not only became dominant over the feminine, but has been abusing and raping her for millennia. Sky god Zeus is the poster boy for unbounded masculine power and control. The earlier myths change with this shifting dynamic. Not only in the later version does Orpheus lose his feminine half, becoming ineffectual as the shaman-priest, he is then torn apart by the deranged aspect of the feminine out of control in Bacchic orgy. Thus, women even end up blamed for his demise.

Being torn apart is also an integral shamanic theme, but there has to be a numinous reconstitution for the initiation to be complete. The Isis and Osiris and Inanna myths are most germanely about reknitting into oneness. Sadly, there is no reassembly for Orpheus, whose bones are scattered, and whose head remains to madly prophesy. Note also the telling shift from the heart of love in the earlier myth, to just the head remaining, spouting away in the dementia characteristic still today. We are aswirl with opinions and thoughts that we think refer to something real *out there,* and the inner journey to what underlies thought is never taken. Orpheus' loss is our loss of Orpheus.

In reality, thoughts can only refer to thoughts. Thoughts are what western spirituality has 'progressed' to. The premise underlying it all has thought as the vehicle to get to the real, to what *is*. No one in science questions this anymore. No one representing orthodox religions questions thought, especially as the written word. Thought has buried insight.

There is dire need to examine our origins for the misty mythic hints that belie the fallacies of progress and evolution, so to find direction back to the origins we must return to, before the expiration date for the possibility of any real healing passes, transmuting medicine to poison. The road seems unretrieveably lost under plastic skyscrapers, droning wars fought for corporate profit, and an environment dying from lethal soot trailing from a sky *we* are now idiot gods of. The only road left is within: it goes nowhere but to itself, the same underworld Orpheus sank to, where he found his wholeness in partnership with Eurydice, restoring his humanity and divinity. Hades and this world have always been exactly the same place.

The Death of Death

There once was a note
Pure and easy
Playing so free, like a breath rippling by

The note is eternal
I hear it, it sees me
Forever we blend
And forever we die

There once was a note, listen…

Pete Townsend, "Pure and Easy"

had i not known
that i was dead
already
i would have mourned
my loss of life

Ota Dokan's tanka death poem, 1486

There is a deceptively simple mantra that manifests from and points toward the heart of *Ṛgvedic* culture. Vedic people left few artifacts, built temporary structures, wrote hardly any linear history; they left us an empty archeology and wide temporal uncertainty. Were they active 4500 years ago, contemporary with (some say identical to) the hydraulically advanced and urbane Indus Valley Civilization? Or even a post-Atlantean backwash much, much older, as some of the Vedic astrology and archeo-geography indicates? Their only viable legacy is aural, a Sanskrit language and collection of poetry dedicated to and sonant with the sacred font of being and creation. Sanskrit is the only ancient language we know the actual sound of, thanks to the generations of dedicated chanters adhering to circuitous sacrificial rituals, whose origins are foggy and drift is obscure.

The word 'Sanskrit' contains within it the root √*kṛ*, which gives us that problematically ubiquitous word, *karma*. Sanskrit most often translates as 'well-made', or 'perfectly-done', which works, as long as we remember that karma originally referred to action done during the sacrificial ritual, long before it was glommed by the Theosophists and given a biblical white-washing. Good karma originally meant a well-performed and efficacious ritual, bad karma the opposite.

Language either has a sacred origin or it does not. Either it evolved from proto-Darwinian grunted utterings, or it came as a gift of the gods—in the case of Sanskrit, the goddess Vāc (pronounced 'vuch'). Favoring the latter possibility, archeology overwhelming demonstrates that civilizations arrive in full flower, followed by a slow declination which nostalgically looks back to that incipient golden age. With language it's the same. The earliest Sanskrit is the most mysterious, elastic, poetic, multivalent, and *alive*.

Sanskrit, the language of Vedic ritual, is 'well-made' from the sacrifice itself, the origin of language. The well-performed ritual connects to this ground of language. Sanskrit emerges from and returns the poet to this ground. The origin of the *Ṛgveda,* the origin of Sanskrit, and the origin of the sacrifice are this same unfathomable root. The result of a 'well-made' sacrifice is the perpetuation of good activity/karma accordant with it.

Sacrifice, from the Latin *sacre,* means 'to make sacred', while *yajña,* the Sanskrit equivalent, in Vedic times included worship, devotion, prayer and praise. All sacrifice is traced from the original sacrifice, that is, the One into the manifest.

Unless the Absolute sacrifices its unity, there can be nothing else. How that happens is the open mystery sung in the 10,800 *Ṛgvedic* poems.

One such song, called the Pavamana Mantra, resounds Vedic wisdom in tiers of nested relationships. The name Pavamana carries the sense of straining something to purify it, as part of the soma ritual. Soma, or what little we know of it, is described as a milky substance that is itself strained, and certainly the first identified and deified entheogen. There is soma the drink, and Soma the lord of the power of the drink. It became scarce even in Vedic times—and we can only throw guesses as to what it was, based on limited descriptions, and by projections backwards from the present based on tribal usage. Such speculation rarely takes into account the entirety of the ritual within which soma was ingested, and normally looks at the isolated physical effects of the plant and the individual experience of the journeyer. But soma was only taken during a ritual, never in isolation, and in that ritual many varieties of priests chanted sustained Sanskrit verses, sometimes for days, while the vibration of that intonation potentized not only the soma, but the also taker of the soma and the witnesses to that sacrifice.

असतीमा सद् गमय

तमसी मा ज्यीतरि् गमय

मृत्यीर् मा अमृतं गमय

Here is the chant under explication:

asatomā sad gamaya

tamaso mā jyotir gamaya

mṛtyor mā amṛtaṁ gamaya

Here is the standard translation:

Lead me from the unreal to the real.

Lead me from darkness to light.

Lead me from death to immortality.

The verb in all three lines, *gamaya*, from the root √*gam*, is the causative tense of 'go', while the *mā* refers to 'me', thus the loose meaning 'causing me to go'. This is really not the same as saying 'lead me', where the speaker is asking for beneficial direction from an outside deity. That is the typical understanding of prayer in most current cultures, through which religion matters little. The tendency is to pray *for*; rarely do we pray *from*. This *Ṛgvedic* mantra is inside the ritual: the chant is descriptive of what the chant does. Intoning this chant, we pray within. The chant carries[1] me from someplace to someplace else. But where?

Three movements—from *asat* to *sat*; from *tamas* to *jyoti*;

1 Thanks to Peter Kingsley's book *Reality* and his translation of Parmenides' poem as an incantatory experience at the foundation of what is now the lost sacred tradition of the West. The word 'carry' is repeated four times in the opening lines to actually transport the listener/chanter to where the poem goes:

The mares that carry me as far as longing can reach rode on, once they had come and fetched me onto the legendary road of the divinity that carries the man who knows through the vast and dark unknown. And on I was carried as the mares, aware just where to go, kept carrying me straining at the chariot; and young women led the way.

from *mṛtu* to *amṛtaṁ*—correspond to three levels of meaning or embodiment: the cosmic, the personal and the community.

Another working translation might serve better at this point:

Carrying me from the unmanifest to existence;

Carrying me from concealment to illumination;

Carrying me from death to the movement of Life.

From *asat* to *sat*

Sat comes from the root √ās, 'be', 'exist', and has a constellation of meanings that include 'real', 'truth', and 'actual'. On one level we are going from non-truth to truth, unreal to real, which sounds like gaining some kind of clarity or knowledge. One of the ten classical Yoga observances, *satya,* is a practice of truthfulness, not in the sense of avoiding the moral shortcoming of falsehood, but to have speech and being at root the same. Gandhi caught the sense of this by calling his project Satyagraha, 'truth-grasping', as a process, a movement.

Then to take the chant deeper, the movement from *asat* to *sat* proceeds from non-being to being. How does 'non-being' make any sense? Can anything not *be*? If we think or say it, it is, even in thought. A better translation for *asat* is 'ground of being', or 'unmanifest', the hidden waters from which all of experience emerges and falls back into, moment by moment. The ocean, the Gnostic pleroma, absolute fullness and potent potential of everything: nothing in fact could be more full.

To approach an understanding of this we need myth, in this case the central *Ṛgvedic* story of Indra and Vṛtra, with help from Soma and Viṣṇu. Remember that real (*sat*) myth lives outside of historic time, and is ever-occurring, not an event in the past done and gone. Isis always reassembles Osiris; Inanna continuously descends to the underworld of her sister, dies and returns; Athena always bursts forth from Zeus, the original splitting headache; and concerning us here, Indra always slays Vṛtra, 'over and over', releasing the waters.

Indra, 14th century.

A particularly powerful *asura*, or evil presence—a snake or dragon of some sort—holds back the waters, or holds back the cows. Its name is Vṛtra, from the root *√vṛt*, which can mean either conceal or turn. Both work here, as the dragon covers the waters by wrapping around them. Indra privileges himself from among the storm deities—his weapon is the *vajra* or thunderbolt—and with the help of Viṣṇu (Viṣṇu's superpower is the ability *to stride*, that is, generate space), grows powerful by ingesting the *soma* he brings. Interestingly, Vṛtra's power to hold back creation also comes from *soma*. Vitalized, Indra slays Vṛtra with the flash from his *vajra*, the waters flow, the cows emerge, and heaven and earth, sun and sky are set. The 'seven pregnant cosmic streams' are released, which could refer to the chakras, or the septet of known tuning systems, as the *Ṛgvedic* mantras are all musical song-poems. They are pregnant because they can birth all the possible *Ṛgvedic* song-poems. The cows are often described as 'loo-ing', indicating the image is associated with emerging sound. And of course, one can invert *moo* to *om*, the absolute origin of all sound.

Soma (from √*su*, 'press') is certainly a mystery, extracted from some plant matter, sometimes depicted as a stalk or called a leafless vine, grown in the Himalayas, milky when pressed out, and scarce even in Vedic times before an unknown substitute was used. It definitely had entheogenic qualities, but these have to be understood in context of the sacrifice. None of the usually proposed plants—*Amanita muscaria* (fly agaric mushroom), *Asclepius acida* (milkweed), or *Ephedra sinica*, for example—are satisfying, and it may be that the original plant/deity pressed served its purpose for a time and is now simply gone.

Several millennia later Indian texts such as the *Yoga Sutras* of Patañjali and *Saṁkhya Karika* of Iśvarakṛṣṇa discuss sound as producing the first element, space or *aka*śa. As sound generates space, they arise simultaneously in experience. The Indra-Vṛtra myth enacts this cosmogonic movement from *asat*, the unmanifest ground of being, to *sat*, a meaningful creation of the cosmos regulated by the sacrificial chant. This proceeds moment to moment, eternal release and reabsorption and release and reabsorption from and back into oneness. This living myth expresses the cosmic level of the Pavamana Mantra.

From tamas to jyoti

The next line of the mantra, going from *tamas* to *jyoti*, darkness to light, works on the level of the *ṛṣi* or *kavi*—the *Ṛgvedic* poet—and the human inspirational aspect. The *ṛṣi* ingests *soma*, and through its power literally becomes Indra. Thus, he re-enacts the myth, and by connecting to the ground of being, *asat*, opens the waters of inspiration that are held in the unmanifest.[2] For the *ṛṣi*, the power of soma released becomes Vāc, the goddess of creative speech, sometimes called 'the mother of the *Ṛgveda*'. The *ṛṣi* in RV 1.164.37 sings:

> Concerning what it is I am, I do not know.
> I wander wrapped and concealed in thought.
> Then Vāc came to me, first born of *ṛta*.
> I received a portion of her.

The poet's own mind, like Vṛtra, conceals his connection to Vāc. She precedes the gods: the vibration of her voice, which is the cosmos-ordering of the *Ṛgveda*, brings them into existence. The poet does not know who he is until he connects with her. Vāc embodies the vibrational stirrings emerging from the ground of being, what later Kashmir Shaivism philosophy calls *spanda*, the initial inchoate quivering and sounding note of all manifestation. The power of the poet, the *ṛṣi*, is the power of Vāc, the power to generate a cosmos through the chant, through the song of poetry. This chant then occasions a cosmos resonant with the *ṛta* from which it comes (*vāc* is also the sound of the pressing stones, connecting this back to the *soma* ritual). *Ṛta* is a close functional correlate of the *logos* of Ancient Greece, the correct ordering of manifest experience in resonance with the chant, resulting in a moral and natural cosmos. The *ṛṣi* becomes Indra, breaking open the sacred springs with the thunderbolt flash of inspiration, then able to put the worlds in order through the song.

2 The Old Testament correlate is *fiat lux*, "let there be light," moving across the waters, which are the ground of being.

And like Indra, the *ṛṣi* must accomplish this over and over in continuous mythic recreation, preventing another static concealment and descent into inertia.

Saraswati, 12th century, Gujarat.

Darkness, *tamas*, conceals and is stuck (from the root √*tam*: 'exhausted', 'suffocated', 'out of breath', 'immovable'). This moves in the chant to *jyoti* (from √*jyut*, 'shine upon'), illumination, wisdom. This movement in the chant occurs within the poet, in simultaneous reenactment of the cosmic movement from *asat* to *sat*, Indra slaying Vṛtra.

The obvious correlate in the West is the *Gospel According to John*, by far the most cosmic of the synoptic gospels, where *logos* functions nearly identically to *ṛta*.

> In the beginning was the *Logos*, and the *Logos* was with *Theos*, and *Theos* was *Logos*...in him was life, and the life was the light of all humanity; the light shines in the darkness, and the darkness did not grasp it. (1.1, 4, 5)

Also in *The Corpus Hermeticum*, where *logos* again equates to light:

> "That light," he said, "is I, *Nous*, your *Theos*, who was before the watery substance appeared out of the darkness, and the light-*logos* from *Nous* is the Son of *Theos*...that which sees and hears within you is the *logos*." (1.6)

So much was lost when unimaginative Roman-Christians concretized *logos* in translation to the Latin *verbum*, thence in the King James Bible to 'word'. That declination of subtlety is responsible for the even more unimaginative biblical literalism ruining far more lives than it has saved. But here in the *arche*, the beginning, where *logos* is still with *Theos*, God-*logos* is the divine formative principle of the cosmos. It contains ratio—thus 'rationality', 'oratorio' and 'reasons'—but which ratios used determine the type of cosmos generated. This comes into play with musical tuning, architecture, and for the Vedic people, construction of the sacrificial altar, where certain ratios are evocative of the divine and harmonize with our human divine aspect. The *logos* generates the blueprint of creation from the place of unmixed light and vibration.

Going back to Vāc, 'first born of *ṛta*', she is at the source of creation, ordering and pervading all of it:

From Vāc flow the oceans,
By her live the four directions
The entire universe stands
on the imperishable vibration flowing from her.
(10.164.42)

I give birth to the father on the brow of the cosmos.
My womb is in the waters of the deep ocean.
From there I spread out over all creatures,
And touch the sky with the crown of my
head. (10.125.7)

Vāc is sound, speech, and language, and as a goddess bespeaking the *ṛta* she orders space and time through the vibration of her speech. She is the inspirational font for the Vedic *ṛṣi*, the *arche* of the entire pantheon chanted into being. And just as light and sound come together in the *logos*, the movement from the darkness of *tamas* to the light of *jyoti* is the speech of Vāc come through the poet's chant, overcoming the inertia of a rigid perspective, a concealment of life by Vṛtra. Through the power of soma, the *ṛṣi* performs the heroic activity of Indra over and over.

This movement is recast in the *Bhagavad Gītā* a few thousand years later. The earliest Sanskrit texts—the *Ṛgveda*, the *Upaniṣads* and the *Āraṇyakas* (forest texts commenting on *Vedic* ritual)—are all classified as *śruti*, or 'heard': not surprising, since the chant brings the cosmos into existence and aligns Vedic culture supernally. This original 'vision' is actually aural. Later texts such as the *Bhagavad Gītā*, *Yoga Sutras*, and the *Purāṇas* (recast myths and cosmogonies), and the epics *Mahābhārata* and *Rāmāyaṇa*, are all considered *smṛti*, 'remembered', a re-membering of that earlier foundational 'aural' vision.

The *Bhagavad Gītā*, currently the central spiritual text for India, tells the tale of the warrior Arjuna, to whom Kṛṣṇa gives a deep extended spiritual talk and vision on the brink of an epochal dharmic battle Arjuna falters in the face of. In a word, this battle is fought over dharma. Dharma is, among many things, the lawful sacred ordering of civilization, a close correlate to Vedic *ṛta*. Arjuna is the son of Indra; Kṛṣṇa is the eighth avatar of Viṣṇu,[3] and Vṛtra amounts to adharma, or 'anti-dharma'. Kṛṣṇa incarnates when there is an increase in this adharma. These characters in the *Bhagavad Gītā* renovate the Vedic myth, acting the same roles. Just as Viṣṇu brings soma to help Indra overcome the concealer Vṛtra, Kṛṣṇa helps Arjuna overcome his inertia, his *tamas*, through the power of the vision he prepares and grants through giving his 'divine eye'. In both cases the result is a culture generated concordant with a sacred vision, expressed through sacred chanted text.

And just as the power of soma later becomes internalized as *śakti* coiling about the spine, Vāc, power of speech, becomes the goddess of music and the arts Sarasvati. In fact, there exists a *soma chakra*, to be meditated upon, midway between the *ājña chakra*, the 'third eye' between the eyebrows, and the *sahasrāra* chakra at the crown of the head. The earliest *śruti*/heard chants ordered the cosmos without, and the later *smṛti*/remembered texts and practices order the same, only within the body of experience. The mystic unifies within and without.

Thus, this *Ṛgvedic* performance is not just for the poet as an individual. In fact, one certainly cannot call a *ṛṣi* an individual in any modern imaginable sense. The *ṛṣi* has an astonishing memory, internalizing probably all 10,800 poems in the *Ṛgveda* and then countless other texts and rituals. His whole sensorium is structured of the bricks of these chants, the vibrations of which have hummed within him since before the beginning of memory. His whole life circles about the continuation and innovation of these chants which structure the sacred life of the *Ṛgvedic* community.

3 Avatars of Viṣṇu one through six are mainly mythological animal deities, seven is Rama, eight is Kṛṣṇa, nine is either Kṛṣṇa's brother Balarama for the orthodox Hindu, or Gautama Buddha. The Buddha is seen either as a bringer of a valid teaching for some, or as a test by Viṣṇu according to some Vedantists to find out who would be duped by such a false teaching. The tenth is called Kalki, a future avatar for the end of this Kali Yuga, for whom there are many current claimants.

<u>*From mṛtu to amṛtaṁ*</u>

The third line of the Pavamana Mantra sings *mṛtyor mā amṛtaṁ gamaya*, usually translated as 'Lead me from death to immortality'. On the surface it seems to make sense. Except that the starting point is death, normally the terminus. It only makes sense reading back from current doctrines of reincarnation or eschatology. But there is little in the *Ṛgveda* concerning the afterlife, and it will be several thousand years before one's reincarnation becomes calcified and predictable through the *Laws of Manu*. In fact, the earliest post-Vedic discussions concerning death, found in the *Bṛhadāraṇyaka Upaniṣad*, ultimately find death's avoidance in correctly chanting and performing the ritual sacrifices. The texts display no interest in some sort of continuous day-by-everlasting-day vampiric immortal incarnation, but rather how to meld with what is numinous and timeless in life itself.

The words *mṛta* and *mṛtyū* (from √*mṛ*—die, decease, be gone) contain the meanings of death, deathlike, departed, gone, stiff and rigid, later to be associated with Yama, the Lord of Death, and cognate with English words like mortician and mortal. Given the other two first terms of this chant—*asat*/unmanifest ground of being and *tamas*/concealment in darkness—there is uncertainty in understanding *mṛtyū* as referring to an individual's death. And since the reading here sees this third section as the Vedic cultural level of the chant, *death* for this culture means an ineffective, torporous chant, one that does not penetrate into the heart of the sounding vision generating it, with Vṛtra concealing it. Death is the dearth of inspiration.

Which leads to a question of where the morphing from this death then goes in the chant. Normally the shift translates as 'from death to a-*mṛta*', literally 'not-death'. *Amṛta* expresses 'immortality', 'imperishable', 'nectar which confers immortality'—soma—and the 'root of a plant', which depicts the unseen aspect producing life on the surface, a metaphor for the occult ground of being. This is a perfectly reasonable translation and works. But we can go deeper and sideways.

In fact, one does not chant *a-mṛtam*, but *am-ṛtam* ('*ṛ*' is a slightly voiced vowel, like 'ri' with a short 'i' and a gentle breath). *Am* means 'go toward', 'sound', 'honor'. This way, following the chant itself, one sings 'toward *ṛta*' instead of 'not death'. Although no one translates it that way, this interpretation follows the actual chant as it is sung. Again, *ṛta* is a foundational *Ṛgvedic* concept. Earlier we saw Vāc, mother of all the Vedic gods, as the *first born* of the *ṛta*, which certainly makes her an early expression out of the unity of the unmanifest.

Ṛta is untranslatable, with some of the attempts 'norm', 'cosmic order', 'world order', 'truth' or 'correct ordering', from the root *√ṛ*, 'go', 'move'. Even more than *vāc*, it measures up to *logos*, and the *tao*. Later *ṛta* gets enfolded into another busy word, dharma, where dharmic activity lawfully (*√dṛ*, 'hold to') abides by the *ṛta*. *Ṛta* as a Vedic concept contains both, this cosmic order and all activity in accord with it. Everything lawful then happens through the *ṛta*. *Ṛta* encapsulates the cosmic, ethical and liturgical correct order, the norm on which Vedic chant hangs. The chant, as sung tones using specific tuning systems, itself creates this ordering of experience.[4]

---

4 Extensive, dense, important work on tuning theory and numbers in the *Ṛgveda* was done by Ernest G. McClain, especially in his groundbreaking book *The Myth of Invariance*.

"The numbers Ṛgvedic man cared about define alternate tunings for the musical scale. The hymns describe the numbers poetically, distinguish "sets" by classes of gods and demons, and portray tonal and arithmetical relations with graphic sexual and spacial metaphor" (p.3).

Chant 1.164 offers many clues:

> The twelve-spoked wheel of ṛta rolls in the sky without diminishing.
> Seven hundred and twenty sons in pairs rest on it Agni. (1.164.11)
>
> Twelve spokes, one wheel, three navels.
> Who has understood this?
> Three hundred and sixty rest on it like poles that do not loosen. (1.164.48)
>
> Seven horses draw the seven-wheeled chariot,
> Sounding seven sacred notes…
> Wise ṛṣis have woven a seven-stranded web about the calf above (the sun).
> (1.164.3,5)

The contrast with Indic traditions as they are marketed here now has the current emphasis on some sort of personal enlightenment: *self*-realization, or an enlightened ego, which from the mystic perspective is an impossibility. The ego *is* the concealer. Unfortunately this is what is left in this broken world where the sounding note of every sacred tradition is unrecognizably distorted by its lost progeny.

The *Ṛgvedic ṛṣi* fashioned new songs over and over, connecting to the original sound-ground, the unmanifest *asat,* through the power of soma. These songs, because of their emergence from the original tone of the Vedic civilization, necessarily express the sacred order of the *ṛta,* and these chants themselves organize experience in accord with it, expressed through the power of divine speech, or the goddess Vāc. This chanting not only structured the experiential body of the *ṛṣi,* but the body of the whole community. It is essential to remember that for the mystic, the body is the unitive entirety of experience, including the senses and the elements felt as 'out there' in what is now ordinary human consciousness.

This is the movement from death toward the *ṛta* expressed in the chant. This is the holding together of sacred community. Death is stagnancy, clinging to immovable rigid perspectives. The *ṛta* is life aligned to the grounding vision enchanted. Global

---

There are often five or six or twelve spokes to the wheel; seven wheels or riders or sisters or sons—remembering that the original creators of Vedic culture are the seven *ṛṣis* forming Ursa Major and their mates, the seven sisters in the Pleiades—with lots of twins and pairings. It takes a mathematician and musicologist the caliber of McLain to unstrand these webs with a ring of truth.

The twelve-spoked wheel, which most will read as the year, can also be the twelve-note scale derived from whole number ratios. Five or seven spokes are the different tuning systems. For McLain, Vṛtra is the undifferentiated pitch continuum that Indra/*ṛṣi* 'slays' to create an original hymn with a particular tuning specific for it. Numbers like the 360/720 pairing reflect the invariant octave, where if one doubles a string length, the same note occurs an octave lower. Halve the string and the note is an octave higher. The ratio of 1:2 (360:720 is the same as 1:2) keeps us with the same note in different octaves. It takes the whole number integer string length ratios—such as 3:2, 4:3 and 5:4, which give the fifth, fourth and major third respectively—to give us music. All of this can only hint at the depth of cosmogenic knowledge embodied in the *Ṛgvedic* hymns and the *ṛṣis* whose vision birthed them.

correlates might be the perpetual Druidic choirs of Britain, the songs holding the wisdom of just about any aboriginal culture, and the katabatic incubational practices of ancient Greeks, connecting to goddesses and gods in underworld stillness, bringing back laws, chants and cures for mortals, cities, and cultures.

Where and how does the sacrifice, *yajña* (√*yaj*, consecrate, worship, very similar to *sacre-facere*, 'make sacred') originate? Even before the sacrifice of Vṛtra by Indra allowing for manifestation, there is the original sacrifice, 'beyond *sat* and *asat*'. The original sacrifice is always the movement of the Absolute to the Ten Thousand Things. The Absolute is alone and wants to be known. A longing desire beats the heart of all creation. In the Vedas they call this *tapas*: heat, friction, vibration. Sound *is* vibration. The Absolute sacrifices absoluteness to allow the many to be. What kind of a cosmos ensues depends on the efficacy of the chanted vibration. A harmonious cosmos sings from a vibration closer to the original note; a violent angry cosmos issues from distortions along the pitch continuum. All sacrifice, any time someone acts selflessly, recapitulates the original sacrifice.

Vedic death is culture not born from the sacred vibrations of the *ṛta*. According to the hymns even the gods become immortal through *tapas*, through sacrifice. The way to go beyond death, as attested to in the texts, is to perform the sacrifice, that is to *live* the sacrifice. Immortality for Vedic people cannot be something as mundane as living linear time without end. It is the continuous merging with the timeless ground of being and emerging from it, over and over, manna baked fresh momentarily.

Germane?

Surprisingly, the language of this mantra remains relevant to Indian culture thousands of years on. A recent example written by exemplary philosopher and environmental activist Vandana Shiva, "The Food Dharma",[5] forms the argument against GMO's in terms of *dharma*, *adharma*, and *ṛta*. For Dr. Shiva, dharma:

5 *The Asian Age*, 10 September, 2015.

> ...signifies the "right way of living", aligned with the *ṛta*—the order that sustains life and maintains the universe...and all creation, from the microcosm to the macrocosm, from the tiniest microbe to the largest mammal...dharma arises from the interconnectedness of all life, and our duty to care for all humans and all species alike.
>
> The opposite of dharma is adharma, the violation of *ṛta*, of the ecological laws of the planet, and of the duty to care for the planet...Whatever separates us from nature and each other, every action that leads to the disintegration of societies and ecosystems is adharma.

Not being 'carried from death toward the *ṛta*', and instead perpetuating inert cycles of stagnancy, sadly describes too well the current farming situation in India. Death is the 300,000 farmer suicides, often by ingesting the herbicides that no longer work on the GMO plants foisted upon them by Monsanto and its ilk. Death is the quality of the produce grown by these poisonous methods, the cancerous termination from eating them, and the toxic run-off no living water supply can avoid. And death is co-option of the divine miracle of the creation process in seed: as Dr. Shiva writes, "Instead of seeing food as the creator, corporations and scientists developing GMO's are taking over the role of 'creator' through 'patents' on life."

These corporations and their government abettors *are* Vṛtra, concealing the waters of life, holding the power of soma for themselves, in spite of the Indra-inspired *ṛta*-guided efforts of Vandana Shiva and her kindred activists.

Corporate Vṛtra is still held together by a chant, by the power of speech, a language distorted from vision to avarice. The chant of corporate media upholds the chant of corporate personhood; the chant of bought scientists whoring their credentials; the chant of legal advertising lies chanting false credence; the chant of wage slavery and institutional poverty;

and the chant of malignant food and industrial pollution sickening billions and funneling them into the chant of the corporate medical profit machine.

There is an original tone, a foundational song to every civilization. Each emerges from the sacred, born of a numinous vision. How can we find that tone for our western culture? At least for Vandana Shiva a living language of *ṛta* and *dharma* exists for her and her culture. It might only be a pale echo of the original chant informing the *Ṛgveda,* but it's still easier to trace these aural tones to their source than in the West. For the West, the only audible sounding tone left lauds the drone of relentless war, the ultimate incorporation of senseless death.

Yet the original tone *has* to still exist, if only because the arias of violence and ego and acquisition need it to exist in order to be an aberration of it. Who has the guts and the desire to do the inner archeology in stillness and silence to hear it?

AI is still artificial

Taking this to yet another level, one of current 'understanding' of the brain, consciousness and artificial intelligence: when 'futurist' Ray Kurzweil joined Google, which then bought a slew of robotics companies, there was only one possible reason. Mr. Kurzweil would like nothing better than to be able to upload his brain—what he thinks is his consciousness—into a machine and live forever: going from death to immortality in the most mundane, egoic way possible.

Another 'prophetic futurist',[6] Michio Kaku, loves AI and its putative possibilities, like recording dreams, experiences and consciousness itself. The essence of their unrealized presuppositions runs thus: when computers were being formulated, basically one thing was known about the human brain: neurons fired or didn't—a binary system. Even the most 'evolved' computers today run on binary coding. As computers became

6 See here the degradation of the original meaning of 'prophet', who is one who can speak for the Divine, understanding the past and future contained in the present moment.

more sophisticated, neurologists were able to use them to model brain behavior on them. Now, AI uses computer models formed on theories of how brains work, which were derived from computers themselves, which were derived from a very basic and incomplete understanding of how brains work. None of it is based on anything real, and all you can get is more and more derivative complex patterns. In other words, Siri will *sound* more and more like how someone *thinks* a human sounds like. In more other words, the brain is *not* a really intricate convoluted computer.

But those are just surface presuppositions, getting away from the fact that no one knows what intelligence is, let alone what a full human is.

And there is more basic presumption to this discussion. Simply put, every prediction of the likes of Kurzweil and Kaku evolves from the premise that our consciousness, memories and awareness all arise from the 'meat brain' and the brain only. Human creativity, emotion and ego, are all the epiphenomena of neurons firing in patterned sequences and amalgams. 'All' we have to do is map the patterning of the brain, replicate the circuitry, and *voila!*—we have conscious AI. This is of course not to deny electro-chemical activity within the brain, of the effect altering that chemistry has on the *experience* of consciousness, but it begs the question of the origin of all experience. For these people it is obvious that experience is exclusively physical.

To the mystic, the Vedic *ṛṣi,* and even the occasional physicist, the inverse is true. Consciousness is prior and gives rise to the gross, the brain included—being carried from *asat* to *sat*. This is not the prediction or theory of the mystics, this is their direct unassailable experience. To reduce their insight to some 'God neuro-receptor' is the ego of science, which subsumes everything to its limited purview. Like corporations, this form of science cannot be satisfied working within the qualified realms in which it can succeed, but hubristically extends itself beyond its relevance. Their adharmic activity does not support the *ṛta,* because they have no connection to the divine sounding that brought even their displaced logic into being. They are not happy making a living; they need to make a killing.

In a full inversion of the myth of Indra slaying the demon to release the cosmic waters, they continuously hold back access to the divine by worship of the material, and Vṛtra wins. And what could be closer to living death than aspiring to have your consciousness transistorized and encased in heavy metal? What sort of *logos* ensues from there?

The way to elude death is not to live forever. The way to trick death is to die before you die, to still the ego out of vibration so that the original note shines forth, singing death's final secret: there is no death.

Yama's dance of death, Mongolia, 18th century.

Hamlet and Arjuna Handle Crisis

"Who are you most like, Lear or Othello?" dropped my college advisor during one of our far-ranging discussions. My immediate response was, "Hamlet."

"That's what everyone says," she replied, and I felt like another sour sucker in a long-running lit gag. Everyone wants to attend *Lear, Othello,* or *Macbeth,* but no one wants to *be* them. The universal appeal and personal connection most feel to Hamlet the character, and what makes him so compelling, is hard to grasp. Not having been raised in India, one imagines a similar relationship people have with Arjuna and Kṛṣṇa, whose mystic conversation comprises the *Bhagavad Gītā*. They stand as pristine paragons of virtue among heroes for Hindus. Yet, like some quantum literature, the more closely we look at them and the situations they face, the stranger and more ambiguous their uncertain worlds become.

Shakespeare's *Hamlet* and India's *Bhagavad Gītā* dwell at the pinnacle of their culture's literary cannons. Although one is dramatic in form and the other considered a sacred text, both articulate human crisis and its unraveling at a radical level. Considering the *Gītā* in its context within the massive epic, the *Mahābhārata,* and not as a separate work,[7] there are striking parallels with *Hamlet*. These similarities in certain ways are microcosmic representations of eastern and western orientation

7 Was the *Bhagavad Gītā* a separate text inserted into the *Mahābhārata* at a later time? There are certain parallels with this epic and the Trojan war cycles of Greece, especially in that they describe wars that end a particular age—the Age of Heroes of Ancient Greece, and the Tritya Yuga (Bronze Age) of Indian cosmology. The name of the 'author' of the *Mahābhārata* poem—Vyasa—means compiler. The best guess is that there were tales about a specific war amongst a family in at least one thousand B.C., and these tales took on cosmic proportions. And as the poem grew, it acquired its own gravitational field, eventually encompassing cosmogeny, and even absorbed the other great Indian epic, the *Raymayana*, into its fold. Whether or not the insertion of the *Gītā* represents a Kṛṣṇa-ization of the epic is irrelevant. Such would just be part of a morphological process that is more or less complete today, and what we have now is what we deal with.

to the Sacred,[8] and in other ways universal. A transcultural juxtaposition might be a useful exploration of how intimately these masterpieces bear on our lives.

Hamlet is, of course, a play, the longest of Shakespeare's, and the *Mahābhārata* is an epic, the longest single piece of literature known. Both are written in metric poetry. A play is a living experience for the audience participant, with

> ...the purpose of playing, whose end both at the first, and now, was and is, to hold as 'twere the mirror up to nature, to show virtue her own feature, scorn her own image, and the very age and body of the time his form and pressure. (III.2.17-20)

In other words, to show us our actual selves. The *Bhagavad Gītā* has the same intent, but by a different method, wiping away transitory illusion until the unchanging part of us stands clear.

The title *Bhagavad Gītā* itself means 'Song of the Lord'. The *Gītā* is chanted, an incanted verse myth. The *Mahābhārata* containing it tells the entire human story; there is nothing that is not in it. Myth is ever-eternal, always happening. *Hamlet* is tragic history, linear time, while the *Mahābhārata* depicts cyclical time, vast ages that emerge and return to their origin in the divine. While the difference on the surface appears to be of an experience that is outer—in *Hamlet*—versus inner—in the *Gītā*—directed, the famous Hermetic maxim 'As above, so below', bears extrapolation to 'As within, so without'. These are mirror paths, outer and inner experiences, with plenty of movement up and down betwixt sacred and mundane.

Hamlet and the *Gītā* are in essence works exploring the

8 'East' and 'West' are terms less geographical now, since desacralized 'western'—i.e. United States and European—materialist hegemony has infiltrated the entire globe. The most obscure aboriginal might wear a Nike cap and garish t-shirt. For the purpose of this article, 'east' refers to a traditional orientation resting on a vision of the divine, while 'western' vision is generally based on an autonomous ego operating in an independently-existing material world.

nature of crisis as experienced within their respective cultures. Crisis is not used here in the etiolated sense promulgated via the corporate news, where every prurient tweet is presented as a crisis of impending international doom, complete with lurid graphics and trumpeting crescendos. Crisis is the spark of friction at the intersection of the sacred and profane, horizontal and vertical, spiritual and material, where we have to daily navigate a world seemingly antithetical to all expression of the numinous, finding what is best to do in the face of the impossible. Doing *what* needs to be done, while perhaps never getting to know *why*. As the ancient Greeks understood, to know what to do you need to know what *is*, and crisis both spurs and bridges us to wisdom.

The idea to see here is, if possible, through task, situation, character interaction and extra-textual investigation, how crisis is portrayed, dissected, and thoroughly resolved in a manner displaying the radical orientation of the cultures generating these texts. There will be contradictions, doubts, and hopefully an insight or three from time reflecting the mirror.

Arjuna Sculpture from Bali.

John Barrymore as Hamlet in 1922.

Juxtaposition

Both Prince Hamlet and Arjuna, the prince whose dialogue with Kṛṣṇa structures the *Gītā*, suffer from indecisiveness amidst a cry to action. They have within them the best and worst of their cultures—they are noble and flawed—and one question will be: does only Arjuna have access to the original vision from which culture itself is generated, and thus the ability to extricate himself fully from his (and our) dilemma? This vision is embodied in Arjuna's chariot driver Kṛṣṇa, the eighth incarnation of Viṣṇu, and the 'Lord' who sings the song of the title.

The dramatic grip that *Hamlet* has on western audiences has remained tense through the centuries since Elizabethan England. Despite countless stagings and a swamp of critical literature, few really seem able to, in Hamlet's own words, "pluck out the heart of my mystery" (III.2.351). This mystery is born of the very nature of human crisis. It is a question of what makes people do what they do, or not do what they must. These murky waters clear somewhat upon examination of the nature of crisis, the standard human condition of disconnect from the sacred, especially the divine feminine.

Hamlet and Arjuna's crises are strikingly similar, given the centuries and continents separating their inceptions. Both are princes who find themselves trapped in horrible circumstance within a decaying world, whose only resolution demands the shedding of family blood. The plots insist they both enact impossible vengeance to reestablish proper order to the kingdom. A Sanskrit word that helps clarify the dilemma for both is *dharma,* loosely translated into English as 'sacred law' or 'duty' or 'cosmic order'. It comes from the root √*dhṛ,* meaning 'to hold', 'hold together', or 'support'. Like most terms used across millennia, its definition shifts according to context or school of thought using it. To find one's dharma is to know what vision to hold to in circumstance.

What dharma itself holds to in the *Gītā* is the *ṛta,* the cosmic order to the movement of life. Kṛṣṇa tells Arjuna: "You need to act considering the holding together of the world" (*loka-saṁgraham*) (3.20). To 'do one's dharma' requires some kind of vision, a radical orientation to *what is*. Traditional culture arises from lives lived through this vision. Dharmic action is thus that which sustains the culture's divine orientation, not the culture of ephemeral trappings. This is the groundwork through which humans live fully in the world.

The world of *Hamlet* overlaps the *Mahābhārata's* often—warring kingdoms, power transference, loyalties, palace intrigue, spying, deceit, otherworldly portents and priests—all standing upon an old sacro-religious underpinning that sounds at best 'out of joint' and at worst out of reach. Prince Hamlet sees that he 'must set it right', do the impossible, restore the Elizabethan sense of harmony and proportion, relink the chain of being to its proper celestial hook.

At the outset of *Hamlet* the prince learns of his task. He must kill his uncle, King Claudius, who has just assumed the throne of Denmark upon the death of King Hamlet, the prince's father. The dead king's ghost returns from the nether regions to inform his son that his death was not naturally caused as everyone supposes, but that he was poisoned through the ear while sleeping. The murderer was none other than Claudius, the king's brother upon whom the elective monarchy subsequently fell. Not only has the throne been usurped via fratricide, but the murdering Claudius soon after married the widowed Queen Gertrude, Hamlet's mother. In those times a marriage between a brother and sister-in-law was considered marginally incestuous. Hamlet had already been melancholic due to this 'o'erhasty marriage', with barely two months between funeral and wedding, and disappointment at being maneuvered out of the Danish crown by his uncle. Hamlet's dharma—his culturally determined course of action—is obvious to both himself and the audience. In case he is unsure, the ghastly apparition of his father is there to remind him: "If thou didst ever thy dear father love—revenge his foul and most unnatural murder" (I.5.23). Hamlet is bound by cultural duty to remove a murderer from the Danish throne, and by family duty to be an avenging son to a wronged father.

There are some icy contingencies that immediately temper Hamlet's resolve. The one mentioned explicitly is whether or not the ghost is actually a demon in disguise sent to deceive him into forfeiting his soul. Another is implicit. The Danish court, even with a fratricidal head, functions well on the surface: foreign affairs are attended to, dispatches are sent, and time is made for inebriated recreation. Any expectation for Hamlet to just burst in, slay the murderer, and announce that 'my father's ghost told me to do it', does the play and Hamlet an injustice. To find his initial delay in vengeance a problem, as so many critics do, is to miss the world the play occurs in.

Prince Arjuna finds himself in similar circumstance that demands a bloody outcome. In a vast oversimplification of the *Mahābhārata*—no one has even lived long enough to fully translate it into English—he and his brothers, known as the five Pāṇḍava Princes, lose control of their kingdom to their cousins, the one hundred Kāurava Princes, for an agreed-to period of time, twelve years, plus one in hiding. This befalls due to a protracted enmity between the cousins, and a particular series of events that leads to the loss of the Pāṇḍava kingdom by Arjuna's eldest brother Yudhiṣṭhira via a shady dice game. Yudhiṣṭhira is the son of the deity Dharma, and has a weakness for dice[9] that he later overcomes.

After this prescribed period elapses, the Kāuravas, who, like Claudius, have been ruling the kingdom fairly and competently, refuse to relinquish the throne to the Pāṇḍavas, and

9 The fondness of Dharma for chance—countering Einstein's God of physics who famously does not play with dice—is fascinating and too far afield of this discussion. Arjuna is the son of the god Indra, the great warrior of the *Ṛgveda*. He and all his brothers are semi-divine. Their mother, Kunti, earned an enchantment as a young girl, through devotion to a sage, that gave her the power to attract whatever deity she called. She would become impregnated, resulting in a child, while leaving her virginity intact each time. There is a very indicative contrast here between the feminine calling upon the gods willingly, resulting in the birth of heroes, and the western Greek foundational myths where gods rape mortal women over and over. While the degradation of the feminine is almost ritualized in the West, the divine feminine held a place of honor in India until recently, though as we shall see later, the seeds of her fall have already sprouted in the *Mahābhārata*.

war becomes necessary to restore the cosmos to its proper order. Arjuna and his brothers' cultural status as *kṣatriyas*—warrior-princes—demands this action.[10] *Kṣatriyas* train much of their lives for battle, and as Arjuna's mentor and charioteer Kṛṣṇa tells him:

> There is nothing better for a *kṣatriya*
> than fighting within the dharma.
> Happy is the *kṣatriya,* Arjuna,
> who meets with such a fight, which
> falling to his lot by good fortune,
> uncovers the gate of heaven.[11] (2.31-32)

Arjuna sees no such golden opportunity before him. Instead, he has particularized his vision into a perspective pitting him against "fathers and grandfathers, teachers, uncles, brothers, sons, grandsons, companions, fathers-in-law and friends" (1.26). He is especially grieved to see his beloved teachers, Droṇa and Bhīṣma, armed against him, allied with his enemies for other reasons of dharma. They were his actual fathers, since his progenitor is the deity Indra. Pain causes his vision to narrow. Whereas he should see himself as a karmically-determined circumstance—all past actions have brought him to this point—that he is responsible for and must act within, he experiences a subject/object dualism placing him wholly within a body that must war against teachers and cousins whom he has known since birth. They exist in separate bodies *out there*. This split into disunion induces the crises of war within and without Arjuna.

This is visually depicted by Arjuna having Kṛṣṇa, as his

10 The deeper back story has the epic beginning with the great Earth Mother goddess tired and overburdened with the multitude of men and their ceaseless petty wars. She calls on Viṣṇu to do something about it. Kṛṣṇa is the avatar of Viṣṇu. To quote the famous second line of Thomas Pynchon's *Gravity's Rainbow*: "It has all happened before, but there is nothing to compare it to now."

11 Translations from the *Bhagavad Gītā* are the author's, with an acknowledged debt to the translations of Winthrop Sargeant and Antonio T. de Nicolás.

chariot driver,[12]—after all the ritual conches have trumpeted chaos—move him into the empty battlefield, the *dharmakṣetre* (the 'field of dharma') between the armies. "Stop my chariot in between the two armies that I might behold the men standing there eager to fight" (1.21-22). In this movement he abstracts, or attempts to abstract, himself from his circumstance, separating the unified moment into a past he has moved away from, and an unfriendly future in the distance he is averse to: (de)positing an isolated individualized self, alone and independent from that circumstance. The mythic space now balloons with his aggrandized sense of self, alone and separate from what *he* must do.

Arjuna becomes overwhelmed with the magnitude of his task, and he coalesces into a body that cannot act. He becomes so rigid, his body quivers with indecision. Circumstance arises through activity and demands response within it. This inability for Arjuna to do so literally shakes him to the core. It is the task of Kṛṣṇa, who is the embodiment of cultural consciousness—the sacred and history incarnate, organizing and giving rise to the manifest world in the present—to move Arjuna's body out of one frozen *as* crisis, into a fluid one concordant with an ontological, hypostatic vision. The whole of the *Bhagavad Gītā* is an enactment of this process, moving Arjuna from a stuck perspective to the ability to discriminate many perspectives; from discriminative knowledge to a direct experience of the radical grounding vision embodied in Kṛṣṇa; and finally into an ability to live through this vision.

Hamlet has no access to a Kṛṣṇa to lead him out of crisis. Instead of the dialog Arjuna has with the divine, Hamlet must work out his action through soliloquy. He lives in a society fraught with dead beliefs and crapulous customs "more honored in the breach than the observance" (I.4.16). The Christian churches may hold political sway, aligned with a monarchy eager to link despotism to divine decree, but excepting the rare mystic who would usually be vilified as a heretic, these

12 Kṛṣṇa as a supreme deity has agreed not to fight in the war, but only counsel Arjuna. His peculiar influence affects the outcome in fascinating ways.

institutions had long been divorced from the original living vision from which they arose.

Wittenberg

If no mystic Kṛṣṇa appears to show Hamlet his radical orientation to his culture, what does inform his life and vision? Hamlet is educated at the University of Wittenberg, often called a center of 'natural' philosophic learning, comprised of classes in Protestant humanism, ethics, logic, natural science and Aristotle. Critics often stop there and say that Hamlet is a man of intellectual speculation, so much so that he cannot act in the face of a gut-wrenching situation. The play is then protracted by his intellectualizations, while the crisis worsens and brutal consequences multiply. He famously accuses his Wittenberg classmate Horatio of being stuck in rationality facing the supernatural—"There are more things in heaven and earth, Horatio/Than are dreamt of in your philosophy" (I.5.165-7)—but it is truly Hamlet whose ability to live is circumscribed by 'godlike reason'. And Horatio has no problem recognizing a ghost when he sees one.

But Wittenberg as a reference point is faceted, reflecting contradictory aspects. One face is the Wittenberg connection with Martin Luther and the Protestant reformation being played out bloodily in Shakespeare's England. Is this an implicit endorsement of the Anglican Church? Or just an insert to earn the stamp of the censors?

Another fascinating connection links to straight science: Danish alchemist and astronomer Tycho Brahe spent some time at Wittenberg just before *Hamlet* was written. He famously made observations of a supernova that Shakespeare would have seen blazing in the night sky as a Warwickshire lad. Bernardo's lines in the opening scene likely refer to this supernova in the constellation Cassiopeia:

> When yond same star that's westward from the pole
> Had made his course t'illume that part of heaven
> Where it now burns… (I.1.36-8)

These words portentously occur just as the ghost appears. In spite of the guiding star known through the Christian birth story, a new star generally forebode dis-*aster*, literally, an 'ill star'. In fact, the coinage of 'disaster' can be traced to just before *Hamlet* in 1598 or so.

Another alchemist and astronomer, and sometime magician, Johan Goerg Faust, called Wittenberg home. His life inspired two classic works of literature, Christopher Marlowe's *The Tragical History of the Life and Death of Doctor Faustus* (first performed in 1594), and Johann Wolfgang von Goethe's *Faust* (1808). Not exactly the stuff of natural science.

A less tangential and potentially spiritually significant aspect has Giordano Bruno teaching at Wittenberg 1586-88, noteworthy because of a tantalizing concordance of Bruno and Shakespeare in London, while Bruno resided at the French embassy 1583 through 1586, something explored fully later in this piece. Thus, Wittenberg as a reference point is more ambiguous than just a cold college of reason. It's a hotbed of revolution, alchemy, and maybe even a little magic.

Head, Heart and Hands

Certain words repeat through *Hamlet*, revealing clues to important themes. An audience, of course, does not have the leisure for literary analysis during a performance, but repetition has a resonant incantatory effect on the playgoers. Three terms especially privilege themselves as pivotal—reason or thought, heart, and hands.

Actors utter the word 'reason' sixteen times throughout the play, 'mind' also sixteen, and 'thought' or 'thinking' thirty-eight. Their preponderance and use make mentation a central motif, and clearly align reason with religion—in fact, God—nature, and self-rulership. Here are some of them.

> You cannot speak of reason to the Dane/And lose your voice. (Claudius—I.2.44-5)

O God, a beast that wants discourse of reason/would have mourn'd longer (Hamlet—I.2.150-1)

And there assume some other, horrible form
which might deprive your sovereignty of reason,
And draw you into madness? Think of it.
(Horatio—I.4.72-4)

...a happiness that often madness hits on, which/ reason and sanity could not so prosperously be delivered of. (Polonius—II.2.205-6)

What a piece of work is a man! How noble in reason! (Hamlet—II.2.88-9)

Now see that noble and most sovereign reason,/like sweet bells jangled, out of tune and harsh; (Ophelia—III.1.146)

Sure he that made us with such large discourse,
Looking before and after, gave us not
That capability and godlike reason
to fust in us unused. (Hamlet—IV.4.38-43)

And thus the native hue of resolution/Is sicklied o're with the pale cast of thought, (Hamlet—III.1.84-5)

Our thoughts are ours, the ends none of our own. (Player King—III.2.195)

My words fly up, my thoughts remain below./Words without thoughts never to heaven go. (Claudius—III.3.97-8)

And there is pansies, that's for thoughts. (Ophelia—IV.5.173)

Why, then 'tis none to you; for there is nothing either good or bad but thinking makes it so. To me it is a prison. (Hamlet—II.2.241-2)

> Whether 'tis nobler in the mind to suffer...
> (Hamlet—III.1.57)

Compare this with the 34 uses of the word 'heart' heard by the audience and thus operative within them. Here are some:

> 'Tis bitter cold/And I am sick at heart.
> (Francisco—I.1.8)

> The head is not more native to the heart,
> The hand not more instrumental to the mouth,
> Than is the throne of Denmark to thy father.
> (Claudius—I.2.47-9)

> But break my heart, for I must hold my tongue!
> (Hamlet—I.3.159)

> Hold, hold, my heart,
> And you, my sinews, grow not instant old,
> But bear me stiffly up. (Hamlet—I.5.94-6)

> Must like a whore unpack my heart with words
> (Hamlet—II.2.542)

> ...and by a sleep to say we end/The heartache, and the thousand natural shocks/That flesh is heir to.
> (Hamlet—III.1.61-3)

> Give me that man who is not passion's slave, and I will wear him/In my heart's core, ay, in my heart of heart, (Hamlet—III.2.62-4)

> O Hamlet, thou hast cleft my heart in twain.
> (Gertrude—III.4.160)

> Or are you like a painting of a sorrow,/A face without a heart? (Claudius—IV.7.106-7)

> But thou wouldst not think how ill all's here about my heart, (Hamlet—V.2.187-8)

> Now cracks a noble heart. Good night, sweet prince, (Horatio—V.2.338)

Add to this some of the dozen utterings of the word 'hands':

> I knew your father, /These hands are not more like. (Horatio—I.2.212)
>
> Hold off your hands! (Hamlet—I.4.84)
>
> And lay your hands again upon my sword. (Hamlet—I.5.80)
>
> Gentlemen, you are welcome to Elsinore. Your hands, come! (Hamlet—II.2.341)
>
> Thoughts black, hands apt, (Lucianus—III.2.233)
>
> Leave wringing of your hands. Peace! Sit you down/ And let me wring your heart; (Hamlet—III.4.35-6)
>
> Eyes without feeling, feeling without sight,/Ears without hands or eyes, smelling sans all, (Hamlet—III.4.81-2)

Clearly, anyone watching the play with a certain focused attention will find these words resonating within. The question remains as to whether they echo a coded esoteric teaching, written at a time when such expression was at the very least frowned upon.

Head, heart and hands traditionally depict a triad of spiritual centers discussed transculturally. As a student Arjuna would certainly have studied and concentrated upon the chakras ('wheels'), the seven spiritual foci experienced just central to the spine, a core aspect of Indian spirituality. Three of them, connected directly to head, heart and hands, are major objects of yogic meditation practice. At the space between the eyebrows, the *ājñā* chakra—popularly referred to as the 'third eye'—rules the head, thought, individual consciousness. The heart chakra (*anahāta*, 'unstruck') is the esoteric seat of the continuous sounding of the eternal *AUM*, as well as divine love. The *maṇipūra* ('jeweled city') is where one 'navel-gazes', known as the *hara* of Far Eastern practices, the seat of activity, hence the association with 'hands'. In *tai chi* and other movement arts, it is the place from whence one moves.

Rosicrucians?

If there is no exoteric cultural support for the kind of grounding vision permeating ancient India available to Hamlet, perhaps there were esoteric groups in Shakespeare's time dedicated to entering the mysterium. Although the evidence is spotty, contradictory, and frustratingly inconclusive, there clearly existed alchemical and Rosicrucian activity in Elizabethan England. According to what is called the Rosicrucian science of initiation,[13] each of the three spiritual centers described above attracts a certain character of seeker according to temperament. The head, or thinking center, results in the knower-initiate; the heart, or feeling nexus, results in the seer-clairvoyant; and the hands, or will[14] center, results in the doer-adept.

A problem looms with this approach. Faced with the impossible situation of trying to ascertain the spiritual degree of Hamlet through the spiritual understanding of Shakespeare—a double-layered conjecture—the best we can do is forage around what is known of the time. To ask 'Who was Shakespeare, and who did he hang out with to come up with what he did?' touches

13 Although there is little in the way of written evidence from Elizabethan time, 20th century mystic and expositor of things Rosicrucian, Rudolf Steiner, terms the head-heart-hands triad 'thinking-feeling-willing', and in various forms they are central to his teaching. Whether or not he is making public old esoteric teachings dating to the emergence of Rosicrucian thought in the English Renaissance is a question left to the reader. What is not disputable is the commonality of these centers in spiritual experience.

14 The word 'will' is spoken 183 times in *Hamlet*, sixteen of those as a noun describing the faculty of intentionality, e.g.: "it shows a will most incorrect to heaven;" "like a neutral to his will and matter, did nothing;" or "Our wills and fates do so contrary run."

on the miasma of the authorship question, but something of the spiritual ambience of the time needs an overview for understanding what *Hamlet* might be about. Before looking at that, how Indian literature views authorship reveals something.

The authorship of the *Mahābhārata* epic is handled mythically, and no one seems to mind. The name of the author, Vyasa, literally means 'compiler', and is likely more of a title than a historical figure. At the genesis of the poem, he contracts a deal with the elephant-headed deity Ganesha. When Vyasa asks the inventor of writing, Ganesha, to take down the *Mahābhārata* poem as he recites it, he agrees on the condition that Vyasa compose continuously without pausing. Vyasa agrees so long as Ganesha comprehends each verse before he writes it down.[15] What can be made of this deal? It may have something to do with Vyasa as an aspect of Viṣṇu guiding one age into the next. Part of this involved the transition from chanted memorized verse to written verse. A whole different aspect of one's sensorium is active in tonal chanting. Traditionally what makes Sanskrit a sacred language is that the vibration of the words are the real essence of what the words express, not just an over-layered description. For example, the Mother Goddess chant—the *devi mantra*—is no different from the Goddess herself. The *devi mantra is* the Goddess herself in vibratory form. And when that chant resonates within the singer or hearer, so does she. Then, it takes another deity, Ganesha, to fully comprehend the chant *before* committing it to the static medium of the page. Ultimately, all Indian literature emerges from divine speech, unclaimed by any individual egos.

15 Vyasa actually inserts himself into the *Mahābhārata* as a character, when seed is needed to continue the royal line. In fact, he is the grandfather to both sides of the battle, sort of. Vyasa fathers Dhṛtrāṣṭra, sire of the 100 Kaurava princes, who is blind because his mother Aṁbikā averted her eyes when the unwashed sage Vyasa came to her. Although the Pāṇḍava brothers all have divine fathers, their earthly foster-father Pāṇḍu was ashen because his mother Aṁbalikā turned white upon encountering Vyasa. Pāṇḍu, while hunting, mistakenly fires an arrow through a copulating deer and stag, who turn out to be a sadhu and his wife in disguise. With his dying breath he curses Pāṇḍu, saying that his next act of love-making will be his last breath. And so it is.

As with the Indian epic, the actual authorship question of *Hamlet* is in one sense irrelevant because the words are the same whoever authored them. The societal situations are very different though. Opposed to Europe, India has a long active tradition of enlightenment as human possibility, woven in the fabric of her culture. Sadhus, *ṛṣis* (priest-poets) and sages occupy every village. We forget that this sort of public acknowledgement only recently migrated to the west. Mysticism in Renaissance England and Europe lived, but in trepidation. Whoever penned it, *Hamlet* was written within a year of the mystic Giordano Bruno's execution at the stake. Anyone claiming to encounter the divine via any road not well guarded and tolled by the Church, or any woman using traditional herbs for healing, risked lethal association with Satan by the inquisitional authorities. Thus subrosa protective societies formed.

Frances Yates tells a beguiling story in *The Art of Memory*, obliquely connecting Giordano Bruno with Will Shakespeare, lighting a glimpse of possibility of them doing esoteric work together. Bruno resided at the French embassy in London from 1583 through 1586, under diplomatic protection. He became part of the circle of, and dedicated works to, courtier and poet Philip Sydney. The circle went by the name of 'Areopagus' (Hill of Mars, where the courts in ancient Athens were). Fulke Greville was Sydney's best friend and biographer. A history published in 1665[16] stated that Greville's utmost desire was to be remembered as the 'Master' of both Shakespeare and Ben Johnson, and as a friend of Sydney. There is not much else to go on outside of imagination as to what being a 'master' here means. Both Greville and Shakespeare hailed from Warwickshire, and Sydney's circle met with Bruno around the time Shakespeare would have arrived in London, so there may have been letters of introduction for the young man seeking his big-city fortune. If nothing else this shows it very possible for Shakespeare to have involved himself in an esoteric circle, and a member of one claimed to be his master.

---

16 David Lloyd's *Statesmen and Favourites of England since the Reformation*.

"Trial of Giordano Bruno," by Ettore Ferrari, 19th century.

What would have been taught in such a group? What we do know is that Bruno taught a hermetic memory system, and that part of this system is the compartmentalization of memory like a theater. Richard Burbage, generally acknowledged as the lead in most of Shakespeare's plays, partnered with his dramatist in the construction of the first Globe Theatre in 1599. For a company required to have a large number of plays at the ready, it makes perfect sense that this memory system was incorporated into the structure of this theater, combining Vitruvian classical design and a Hermetic framework. Thus we can imagine a thread from Bruno through Greville to Shakespeare, recalling Hamlet's pun-gent act one line about remembering his father's ghost "while *memory* holds a seat in this distracted *globe*."

There were other esoteric avenues for a real William Shakespeare from Avon to traverse in London. Freemasonry formed in 16th century Scotland, from whence came King James I, eventual patron of Shakespeare's players. The two pillars on the Globe Theatre stage very likely represent Boaz and Jachin, the highly symbolic columns central to Masonic gatherings. But over all these Rosicrucian and Freemasonic considerations shadows the mysterious figure of John Dee

(1527-1609), Pythagorean mathematician, Hermetic philosopher, alchemist, court astrologer, discourser with angels, and the putative model for Prospero in Shakespeare's *The Tempest*.

Dee's life is far too long, wide and complicated to detail here. Its central theme was a sincere attempt to universalize the essence of his time's wisdom to transcend all the warring divisions of religions and countries defining the day.

> While the visit of Bruno brought a strong new infusion of Hermetic influences into Shakespeare's England...a native Hermetic magus had long been highly influential in the Elizabethan age. This was John Dee, a magus formed on Agrippa's occult philosophy and who associated Hermetic tradition with the strong development of mathematics.[17]

Is there some tangible connection between Shakespeare and Dee? Or at least a plausible one? In the diaries of John Dee, he discusses his courier Francis Garland, an obvious pseudonym. In recent years a few researchers[18] have correlated the otherwise unmentioned Garland with the years of Shakespeare's life for which there is no historical contradiction to each of their whereabouts and movements. In other words, no evidence places Garland, a part time spy for Dee, and Shakespeare in different places at the same time. To consider that Will Shakespeare could have been a spy is not much of a stretch. In fact, who wasn't a spy in Elizabethan England? Although this hypothesis can neither be proven nor disproven, it gives the country boy Will access to one of the greatest private libraries in Europe, access to Dee's alchemical and hermetic esoterica, and the ability to enjoy the practical wisdom and travel throughout Europe that are evident in the plays attributed to William Shakespeare of Avon.

---

17 Francis Yates, *Shakespeare's Last Plays: A New Approach*.

18 For example, Teresa Burns' *Frances Garland, William Shakespeare, and John Dees' Green Language*.

"John Dee Performing an Experiment before Queen Elizabeth" by Henri Gillard Glindoni, late 19th century.

The only real evidence of a Shakespearian wisdom is staged in the plays. Does the poetry resonate with some deeper understanding, an attempt by some one or group to externalize and revivify the Mysteries? Frances Yates thought so. She

> began to realise what his (Shakespeare's) great *impresa* was—the dissemination of a magical philosophy which should do away with all religious differences on a level of love and magic—Shakespeare seemed to join that journey to the Supper Party.[19]

Excursis

At this point it may be illuminating to take an excursion into two Temenos Academy lectures given in London in the early 1990's, both on *Hamlet*, both by towering scholars of the sacred, which are nearly antithetical compelling—and problematic—readings of the play. This is a vaguely precarious journey, through thickets of paradox, exfoliating surfaces of what one

19 Yates, *Shakespeare's Last Plays*.

thought was true about beloved characters. Can one live within an ambiguous web of connections?

Martin Lings, well-known traditionalist writer on sacred art, Sufi scholar and author of the landmark book on esoteric Shakespeare, *Shakespeare's Window into the Soul,* gives one talk. The other is by Joseph Milne, lecturer at the University of Kent on Greek philosophy of nature, medieval Christian mysticism, and Shakespeare and Renaissance Christian Platonism. He is the author of *The Mystical Cosmos* and *Metaphysics and the Cosmic Order*. The cruces of their arguments are fueled by varying conceptions of what vengeance means in the context of Shakespeare's writing.

Both readings connect *Hamlet,* as is obvious from Shakespeare's internal clues, with the Edenic fall. The ghost of King Hamlet informs his son: "'Tis given out that, sleeping in my orchard, a serpent stung me...But know, thou noble youth, the serpent that did sting thy father's life now wears his crown." For Lings, this explicit association of the usurper Claudius with Satan is essential. The murder was committed in a fruit tree-laden garden. Claudius eventually admits that his crime "has the eldest curse upon it"—that is primal fratricide by Cain of Abel. When Hamlet tells Ophelia, "virtue cannot so inoculate our old stock but we shall relish of it," Lings sees more than just a prelude to his line "we are arrant knaves all," which on the surface means that Ophelia shouldn't trust any man, including him, and could better live out her life in a cloister. Marrying virtue—that is, Ophelia's virtue grafted upon Hamlet's stock—will come to nothing, it will not take. Lings extrapolates further and sees the key to an esoteric secret:

> Initiation into the mysteries is nothing more than the inoculating or grafting of a scion of man's primordial nature onto the old stock of his fallen nature, which will thus be effaced, stench and all...[20]

20 Martin Lings, Shakespeare's *Window into the Soul*, p. 20.

Lings' premise here demands this initiatic grafting via the sword of revenge. Metaphoric difficulties ensue, as one does not graft with a sword, which cuts entirely, engendering sucker shoots of the same old root stock, but rather with a precise paring knife, followed by binding until the wound heals. Beyond that, the root for Lings is still humanity's fallen nature, and why would you graft what is primordial upon tainted old stock? Shouldn't the primordial be the base upon which to graft your life?

For Lings,

> This complete reversal of the Fall is precisely what is meant according to the play's deepest meaning, not only by "revenge" but also by "honor"...no revenge, no honor.[21]

Thus the slaying of the serpent or dragon overcomes original sin: Hamlet must slay Claudius for spiritual progress. For Lings, vengeance is endemic to spiritual warfare, a language echoed in many traditions. Samurai vengeance stories are legion; for the Prophet of Islam the greater jihad is the struggle within oneself; Arjuna in the *Bhagavad Gita* equally battles his anger, passions, and sense of egoic agency, as well as the Kaurava army, in order to do his dharma.

Joseph Milne sees a fall also, but he is unconcerned with original sin. His reading has Hamlet *descending* through states of being until he drops low enough to embody vengeance, accounting for the oft-remarked 'delay' in killing Claudius. Even if the Old Testament Lord doth claim it for himself, for Milne, vengeance is fully antithetical to the Christian ethos of love and forgiveness displayed in the Gospels, as difficult to enact as they are. This kind of Old Testament jealous God versus New Testament loving Father disputation goes back at least to the second century Anatolian Gnostic Marcion. He produced the first Christian canon, including his own work *Antitheses*, contrasting the Old and New Testament deities with numerous examples. Such as,

21 Lings, p. 21.

the prophet Elisha having the Lord send two she-bears to maul forty-two children because of their heinous crime of calling him "Baldy!" (2 Kings 2:23-24); opposed to Jesus' "Let the little children come unto me, for the kingdom of God belongs to such as these" (Luke 18:16). The Old Testament *lex talionis*, 'An eye for and eye', versus 'If someone smites you, offer the other cheek', is more germane to this discussion.

Milne sees Hamlet facing this choice of vengeance or Christian forgiveness. (There is a third intermediate option for Milne: justice.) These are personified by the Ghost and Ophelia respectively, the former echoing hell and bringing on the unraveling of fate and a resumption of Old Testament virtues; the latter exemplifying Platonic Love, Beauty, redemptive Grace, heaven, and the New Testament covenant.

> When heaven is chosen, then Grace, the power of love and regenerative mercy, enters the play and establishes the Divine Order or ushers in a new Golden Age. When hell is chosen, then Fate, the power of chaos and destruction, enters the play and reverses the order of nature or ushers in an age of darkness and death.[22]

For Milne, Shakespeare's art shines through each character's utterances, emerging from and reflecting his or her state of being. Hamlet cannot exact revenge until he has sunk low enough, due to his refusal of the grace of Ophelia's love. More on this anon. The initial question here is how can such incompatible views of *Hamlet* be true to the play? Is Hamlet redeemed through spiritual initiation, or a damned soul rotting with the state of Denmark?

One of the things that makes Milne's argument compelling is that *Hamlet* is indeed a tragedy. No one rejoices after Act V. No one questions the moral descent of Othello, of Lear, or of the lead in the Scottish play. They are all clearly noble *and*

---

22 Joseph Milne, "Hamlet: The Conflict Between Fate and Grace." All quotes from Milne are from this talk.

flawed—jealousy, arrogance, and ambition grapple with their virtues. The heart of Hamlet's mystery lies deeper. Is 'inability to act' or 'procrastination' a tragic flaw? Or as Laurence Olivier famously and flippantly voice-overed in his film version: "This is the tragedy of a man who could not make up his mind." That would be unworthy of the greatest writer in English. To be a tragedy there has to be a declination, an inexorable sinking, either through fate, character, or both.

According to Milne we identify so strongly with the noble Hamlet (as I did opening this essay), "the divine element in his spirit," that critics miss his fallen soul.

> Confounding the "actual" with the potential Hamlet, they see him as the innocent victim of a cruel Fate over which he has no power or choice. There is a sort of truth in this, in that it corresponds to Hamlet's own view, but I shall argue that Hamlet did have the choice to submit to fate or not and that the option of regenerative Grace was open to him but that he rejected it.

Hamlet's inability to act, in Milne's reading, stems from the fact that he just hasn't fallen far enough throughout the play in order to act with vengeance. Even up until the scene where Claudius is kneeling unable to pray, redemptive Grace can enter and reverse this fall. It's not a matter of delay but descent. Otherwise you have to view *Hamlet* as a tragedy—the full title is *The Tragical History of Hamlet, Prince of Denmark*—not in the classical sense, but in the modern sense of the alienated hero.

In order to comprehend what Milne sees as Hamlet's options, one has to view the ghost of King Hamlet as representing damnation, or Fate. Because the Ghost slinks away upon the hour of the cock, "Shakespeare obviously intends us to understand the Ghost has no heavenly associations." Thus the choice of Prince Hamlet siding with vengeance/Fate as opposed to Ophelia/Love/Grace becomes potential.

"Visão de Hamlet" by Pedro Américo, 1890, Pinacoteca do Estado de São Paulo.

Martin Lings has a very different understanding of the Ghost. Dead King Hamlet is at once "past perfection" and "symbol of man's lost Edenic state." Yet he is also a purgatorial pilgrim and he who "initiates Hamlet into the Mysteries by conveying to him the truth of the Fall not as a remote historical fact but as an immediate life-permeating reality."

Complicating any easy reading is, biblically speaking, that it is not actually Satan slithering in the Garden of Genesis, but the 'most subtle' of God's creation, the serpent. The serpent even closely mirrors Lings' initiating Ghost, as through him Adam and Eve's "eyes were opened" to knowledge. As God says, "Behold, man has become as one of us, to know good and evil" (note the *us*). The serpent performs the same initiatory activity as the Ghost, opening the eyes of Adam and Eve, and Hamlet respectively, to the truth of what is really going on. The barely justified punishment given to Adam, Eve, *and* the serpent gives Gnostics like Marcion plenty of reason to doubt that the Old Testament god and the loving Father of the Christ are remotely the same.

Is the Ghost an initiator, a symbol of past perfection, or a messenger from Hades? Then, is fratricidal Claudius Satan personified?

The underworld connections that trouble Milne, thus undermining for him the Ghost's integrity, are actually proof for Lings that his salvation is assured. To be purging sins is to be on the way to heaven. Given that the entire action of the play spirals from the Ghost's appearance, what he really is, is crucial.

Yet, the events of the play and words of the Ghost make it hard to defend aspects of Milne's position.

> Doomed for a certain term to walk the night,
> And for the day confined to fast in fires,
> Till the foul crimes done in my days of nature
> Are burnt and purged away… (I.5.13)

The Ghost is beyond doubt a denizen of Purgatory: he actually uses the word 'purged', and there is a set duration to his torment, not an everlasting punishment. And who else but Heaven would set those terms? There must be some 'association' then, whereas Milne thinks there is none.

An allusion to Purgatory is all the more interesting because any direct mention of it on stage rendered a play liable to censorship. Reformation theologians actually 'eliminated' Purgatory the year before Shakespeare's birth. Its very 'ghostly' appearance in the play also lends some credence to the scholars who find ties with Shakespeare and his family to the 'old' religion of Catholicism.

Shakespeare technically leaves the question open to the audience as to whether the "airs from heaven or blasts from hell" accompany the Ghost until Claudius' confession and the play-within-the-play. What the Ghost wants helps indicate who he is (anecdotally Shakespeare himself performed this role). He asks first for vengeance, and then for remembrance. Even though the call to avenge his "most foul murder" rings loudest, he also spends many of his lines in concern for his queen.

Being remembered certainly qualifies for a classical definition of a hero's most desired desserts. Little is mentioned about King Hamlet's 'pre-play' life besides the warrior exploits: he has killed King Fortinbras of Norway (of the Fortinbras mirrors later) in battle and taken some of Norway's land. We know nothing else of that conflict. He's committed unnamed "foul crimes in my days of nature," earning him the fires of penitence. He is still a sucker for Gertrude, wishing her no suffering other than her own conscience and the recompense of heaven's justice. Being remembered is, of course, all a classic hero can hope for. The Ghost is certainly concerned with re-establishing a rightful kingship in Denmark, but equally he wants his biography corrected and restored. He exits invoking "Remember me." For Milne, though, the salient quality of the Ghost is his call for vengeance, and the resonance therein with the Old Testament deity.[23]

What of the Ghost's full head-to-toe armor, "cap-a-pe"? Since Shakespeare has Hamlet ask Horatio to reiterate this

---

23 The ancient Greek consideration of memory as the operative aspect of knowledge—literally, truth in Greek, *aletheia*, means not-Lethe, the river of forgetfulness in Hades—doesn't seem to concern Milne the Platonist. Remembrance comes closer to Ling's focus on the wisdom imparted by the Ghost. Although neither thinker mentions remembrance in their writings, it is obviously important to the Ghost himself.

armoring aspect, it might be important.[24] What need would a spirit have of metal encasing in purgatory? The most apparent guess is that his 'crimes' had to do with waging of war, and the killing of King Fortinbras, even though the play explains that these Kings of Norway and Denmark engaged in a legally ratified winner-take-land mano-a-mano honor battle. The karma of this fight is being played out as the play begins, with King Fortinbras' son of the same name building a host of "lawless resolutes," preparing to retake from Denmark what his father lost.

Shakespeare has the entire cosmos of the play cast martially. The sun itself readies for battle: "But look, the morn in russet mantle clad/walks o'er the dew of yon high eastward hill." There is "daily cast of brazen cannon/And foreign mart for implements of war," and excitement in the Danish court as Claudius shrewdly prepares for conflict with young Fortinbras' "unimproved mettle hot and full," while simultaneously using diplomacy to defuse the conflict and redirect his hostility, a tactic he repeats later with Laertes. Contrast this with Hamlet dressed in melancholic black, self-absorbed and ruminative. Shakespeare's brilliance in this juxtaposition of inner Hamlet and outer Denmark eventually resolves to complete expression in the prince's behavior. Hamlet shifts from belligerency to inertia, displaying close to bipolar behavior as his foci vary from inner questions to outer promptings and back.

---

24 As an aside, it is interesting that Horatio recognizes the Ghost's armor as exactly what he wore in combat with King Fortinbras, and he recognizes his frown as the one when "he smote the sledded Polacks on the ice." Horatio says "I knew him," and combined with the above, this would indicate an intimate relationship with King Hamlet, at least visually. Thus he would have witnessed at least two battles. Yet later he says that he "met him once." Very odd. This also begs the question of whether Prince Hamlet attended these battles. Another thing that has always been bothersome is that Hamlet and Horatio greet each other in act one as if they haven't seen one other in some time. How could Horatio be in Elsinore for both King Hamlet's funeral and the coronation and wedding of Claudius a month later, and not have encountered his best friend? Apparently, even Shakespeare needed an editor.

In fact, we can't even tell what Hamlet really thinks of his father. Is he just a man, or a Hyperion deity? Certainly one would expect a number of hairs to jump up upon encountering a ghost, but there is nothing in Hamlet's reaction indicating any joy in reconnecting with a doting father—his only fond memories are of the court jester, Yorick. He even calls the dead king "old mole." And the lack of feeling is mutual. The Ghost only cares to have Hamlet do his bidding. Hamlet's melancholy appears to be less grief than this of his own admission: thwarted ambition from not being elected king, something he could reasonably expect as the son of the past king. Add that to Uncle Claudius marrying mom, and Hamlet is marginalized at the court of Elsinore.

This illustrates the depth and difficulty of coming to an easy reading of who the Ghost is for the play, a character with only a handful of lines. One either takes an interpretive stand—as in Milne and Lings' incompatible interpretations—or wanders Elsinore indeterminate. Any reading becomes more convoluted looking at the more central character of Ophelia.

At least more central for Milne. Lings writes "*Hamlet* is not a drama of love, but of spiritual warfare, of renunciation, and of death and rebirth." (32) "Ophelia personifies all the love and happiness that Hamlet has sacrificed in this life with a view to the next life wither she herself has already been transferred before the end of the play." (53) For Lings, Ophelia is the worldly joy that Hamlet must renounce to undertake this spiritual martial quest of avengement.

Milne differs completely. He has it that Ophelia's love *is* the spiritual quest that Hamlet renounces.

> Ophelia, like so many of Shakespeare's heroines, symbolizes Absolute Beauty in the Platonic sense. She also symbolizes Hamlet's spiritual essence, or his true self, that is to be described in the ascending path of Love described in Socrates' final speech in the *Symposium*...It is through this Absolute beauty, and

> the inspired Love it awakens in the soul, that Shakespeare marries the Christian and Platonic traditions.

She is the 'angel of his better nature', the remembrance of his soul's knowing through Grace and Beauty, the possibility of overcoming sin through virtuous action.

But is she? The action of the play has it that Ophelia rejects Hamlet before he her. Her brother Laertes warns her not to "lose your heart, or your chaste treasure open/To his unmastered importunity," after which her father, Polonius, commands her: "I would not...from this time forth have you so slander any moment leisure/As to give words or talk with the Lord Hamlet." She obeys without demurring: her love crushed, and her fate sealed.

During the scene where she returns Hamlet's letters, while Polonius and Claudius overhear unseen, she herself hides behind a label of honesty, and then lies about where her father is. Hamlet must be able to see the nosey Polonius in order to ask the question, "Where's your father?" in testing her. The point here is not to demean poor Ophelia—she certainly suffers enough—but to show that early in the play she might not be quite the apotheosis of Love and Grace for Hamlet to choose, as Milne states. For in fact, could true love reject her beloved? Would Juliet shun Romeo, following filial duty over Love?

Or, does Hamlet even have the choice between redemptive grace and fated requital Milne says engenders his downfall? Imagine that Hamlet overcomes Polonius' misgivings of his love for Ophelia, and then manages to forgive Claudius in the name of Christian Grace. In what cosmos is it correct for Hamlet and Ophelia to marry and raise little princes and princesses while knowing that a regicidal murderer rules Denmark? In the Yoga system that informs the *Bhagavad Gita*, *himsa*—harming, violence—encompasses not only the actual act of violence, but also thinking about the act, and even approving of the act. Once played out, there is a blurry line between forgiveness and abetting.

"Ophelia" by John William Waterhouse, 1910.

It's hard to acknowledge that Hamlet's treatment of Ophelia gives any indication of real abiding love. His love for her is much like his hot and cold drive for vengeance. He writes lovely poetry, then treats her dismissively and consigns her to a nunnery (also a term in that day for a brothel), then sits atop her provocatively at the play-within-the-play ("Lady, shall I lie in your lap," with a possible pun with 'lie'; certainly 'country matters' is ribald comment meant to send the cheap seats guffawing), then jumps into her grave to wrestle Laertes in vying "tow'ring passion(s)." By that point of the play his "Seems, Madam? Nay it is. I know not 'seems'" seems less seemly.

Not to cast aspersions on poor Ophelia, or even Hamlet, but the play depicts "something rotten" to the core. Nothing is pure, nothing is true, and in the face of this, is anything redeemed?

The question of why Hamlet does not just kill Claudius at the outset has an easy possible answer. Hamlet is ready to kill his father's murderer, "swoop(ing) with wings as swift as meditation or the thoughts of love," *until* he learns it is his uncle, the current king, he must slay. Although Hamlet never fully explains it in a soliloquy, it is fair to assume the average Elizabethan theatre-goer could figure out that a prince cannot just murder a king, and then announce that a ghost told him to do it. The task is not only to rid the throne of a usurper, but to restore it to a rightful state. Not only is there a cunning serpent on the throne, but he is backed by his cronies, especially Polonius. Yet Milne writes: "If 'true kingship' has been usurped through Claudius' murder, then Hamlet's 'spiritual duty' lies in the restoration of true kingship, not in revenge." With Claudius on the throne true kingship is impossible, and Hamlet cannot unseat him by means of 'spiritual' forgiveness. If forgiveness is really not operatively possible given the parameters of the play, there are only justice and revenge left. And all of these result in death.

Before arriving at some sort of conclusion to this foray, there is the 'minor' character of Fortinbras to consider. Again Lings and Milne have deeply opposed interpretations of his role. "Fortinbras represents the perfection that is to come" (23), writes Lings, and Hamlet's encounter with Fortinbras' army about to engage bloodily over a worthless rocky piece of land is "nothing other than a grace" (46), as Fortinbras (alike to Laertes) "personifies those qualities that are as yet virtual in Hamlet and of which the development is an essential aspect of the main theme" (52). And what is the quality that the prince needs to develop along this spiritual journey of his? "From this time forth,/My thoughts be bloody, or be nothing worth!" (IV.4.65-66).

According to Lings, Hamlet has achieved a certain one-pointedness in his heart, whereas previously:

> Thus conscience doth make cowards of us all,
> And thus the native hue of resolution
> Is sicklied o'er with the pale cast of thought,
> and enterprises…lose the name of action. (III.1.83-87)

And this resolution that Hamlet acquires reflects a spiritual advancement:

> Shakespeare is in line with the whole ancient world in assigning resolution to the Heart. Intellect and resolution, the crowns of intelligence and will respectively, are both, according to the esoterisms of West as well as East, enthroned in the Heart, the gateway to the spirit, the "narrow gate" which alone allows passage from this world to the beyond.

Once again, Lings' supposition has bloody thoughts pump through a mystical Heart, and the path of vengeance overlaps the path of the mysteries.

Of course Joseph Milne sees an entirely different Fortinbras than Martin Lings' "perfection that is to come."

> Fortinbras of Norway represents the condition of "lawlessness" that imperils Denmark…In its univer-

> sal sense, lawlessness is the opposite pole to "true kingship", and so represents the ever-present peril to man...The outward resolution of the play is the fall of Denmark to Norway...rule by a "foreign" power, and therefore signifies a fall to a lower order, perhaps a fall from one of the Four Ages to another...there is an outward correlation between Denmark and Norway and an inner correlation between Hamlet and Fortinbras. They are linked by Fate.

Fortinbras of Norway is obviously linked to things bellicose. To give him his due, it is true that he threatens Denmark with 'lawless resolutes' as the play begins, but thereafter he keeps to his word by heeding his own uncle, and channeling his drive to reclaim what his father, King Fortinbras, lost to Hamlet's father, into a pointless war against Poland. Fortinbras does undergo a kind of shift, a maturing, but is still all about war. He orders a martial funeral for Hamlet, whom he has never met, and has hopes of being elected king of Denmark, abetted by Hamlet's dying vote. The final act, where the court has become bloodied with the bodies of Claudius, Gertrude, Laertes and Hamlet, elicits the remark, "Such a sight as this/Becomes the field, but here shows much amiss" (V.2.406-7), as even the soldier Fortinbras finds it hard to fathom.

Thus for Milne, at the end of the play, Denmark is taken further down a belligerent path and handed to Fortinbras, a man who will risk his men for a worthless piece of land, and the cycle of violence is fated to continue:

> But the battlefield is symbolic of the realm of Fate where disharmony, strife and mutability reign, not "true kingship", Love, honor and Grace, symbolized in royalty and the royal court. But since these qualities have been negated, the royal court has become the battlefield of Fate, and thus the rightful kingdom of Fortinbras.

Milne sees Denmark fated to a cycle of violence "with vengeance lord where Grace should rule, death where life should be."

Lings' statement that "Hamlet's fulfillment of his pact (with the divine to be resolute) lies in his perpetual preoccupation with 'honor' and 'revenge'" couldn't be farther from Milne's depiction of a lost Danish cosmos. Neither of them find an ambiguous Hamlet entering the final scene, yet the play obligates a look at the possibility. Yes, there is an acceptance of death in Hamlet's "the readiness is all" speech, and for Lings:

> To be ready for death when it comes is all that matters...Hamlet tells us he himself is ready...
> As such, he is spiritually even more magnetic than before... (47)

But, making the case for Milne's 'lost noble soul' Hamlet, going into the last scene, actually mocks Laertes, someone he supposedly considers noble. His third-person apology for killing Laertes' father Polonius—"Who does it then? His Madness."—is a tour de force of twisted disingenuous logic. Hamlet may be distracted, but he knows he is not mad. He lies to Laertes, then just goes along with the fencing program established by Claudius, and only takes action himself when events—basically Laertes' conscience getting the better of his superior swordsmanship—leave him no other choice. Is this a spiritually resolute proactive pilgrim focused upon 'honor and revenge', or a reactive man still willy-nilly blown about by Fate?

This excursion is not designed to disparage Lings' and Milne's reading by finding where their statements do not correlate with the activity of the play. I have the utmost respect of and enjoy their work immensely. The aim is to give a taste of how dense, difficult, elliptical and impossible to read *Hamlet* is, and their antipodean readings at least attempt to carve the thicket. Is it a flaw, or a measure of artistic brilliance, that almost anything you can say about *Hamlet* generates an equally possible and impossible obverse?

Martin Lings himself addresses this interpretive morass by deferring to the classic Dantean four levels of explication. They go by a number of names and shadings, and Lings' delineation is as good as any:

> Dante mentions the different meanings of a work of art, literal, allegorical, moral, anagogical, in an order that rightly suggests a hierarchy, leading up to the anagogical or the esoteric meaning that is the highest. As to that which comes second to it, the ethical aspect of dramatic art may be said to concern the spectators insofar as they are drawn to identify themselves, in varying degrees, with whatever increase of beauty of soul is set before them on the stage, and to dissociate themselves from all movements in the opposite direction. (25-26)

The greatest works of art synchronize all four meanings. If a play only has meaning on an esoteric level that negates the moral level, should it be knocked off its pedestal as the greatest play ever composed in English? If great art, it is polysemous, of many senses, that operate in concert. Lings admits that Hamlet's failure to kill Claudius when he sees him attempting to pray only fits an esoteric reading.

> Occasionally there are things which don't make sense except at the highest (esoteric) level, for example, take Hamlet's speech, when he fails to kill the king... it's a wonderful opportunity to kill him, but Hamlet always finds arguments to put off what he needs to do, and he says, "Supposing I kill him now, and he is praying, how does that avenge my father?
>
> He expresses, literally speaking, the desire to send Claudius to hell. Well, literally speaking, that is a monstrous idea, it doesn't make sense because it

> doesn't correspond to Hamlet's greatness of character he has because the king, Claudius, did not want to send his father to hell, he wanted the throne, but he didn't want to send King Hamlet to hell. Here is Hamlet wanting to send a soul to hell—a monstrous thing...According to the allegorical meaning, it also doesn't make real sense, certainly not at the moral meaning, but it does make sense at the anagogical meaning because what Claudius represents anagogically is the hold that the devil has upon the soul... and Claudius represents the hold that the devil has on Hamlet's soul which prevents him...something of Hamlet himself, he can send that to hell, that's part of his true character. It is only at the highest sense that that remark of Hamlet, or that attitude of Hamlet, makes real sense. (video)

It's a little difficult to follow Ling's logic here, since if Claudius personifies the grip of the devil on Hamlet's soul, what difference would it make whether that hold is slain and released at any different point in the play? It seems he is just pointing to the only way of understanding Hamlet's attitude, not exactly befitting a great soul, of condemning another soul to eternal torment.

Dante himself wrote in his letter to Cangrande della Scala, "the moral sense, it means to us the conversion of the soul from the struggle and misery of sin to the status of grace."[25] Grace, and the moral meaning of the play, are utmost for Milne, and especially this scene with Hamlet's sword drawn while Claudius kneels:

> It is a decisive moment for them both. Had Hamlet not rejected the path of Love, he could have been at this moment the agent of Claudius' redemption. If *Hamlet* had been a comedy this moment would certainly have been a critical moment when Grace would

25 Translation by James Marchand of the University of Illinois.

> have entered the play and turned it in a wholly new direction. But Hamlet's heart is set upon revenge, not mercy, not even justice.

Hamlet decides to wait until Claudius is sinning—"Up, sword, and know thou a more horrid hent"—thus, according to Milne, negating "the path of regenerative Grace (that) was a possibility for Claudius." This ethical reading of the play apparently makes sense; otherwise one has to explain away Hamlet's monstrous intention as deep esoteric allegory by the author.

The flaw in Milne's reading is that Hamlet becomes solely responsible for Claudius' redemption. Claudius may experience at least a pang of guilt, "Yet what can it when one can not repent?" Still, who the hell is Hamlet to send anyone to Hades? In any reading, that is between God and Claudius. We are left with the real possibility of a Hamlet with a soul so degraded that he relishes the power of damning other souls. This is not his father the Ghost's intent, even if he was "sent to my account with all my imperfections on my head."

Muna Al-Awan, in her perspicacious article based on years of teaching Shakespeare to students interested in his sacred orientation,[26] understands well the multi-faith concept of 'spiritual warfare', echoed by the famous *Hadith* of the Prophet of Islam: "We go from the lesser struggle to the greater struggle," that is, from an external battle to the infinitely more difficult struggle within ourselves. Also, in the *Bhagavad Gītā*, Kṛṣṇa tells Arjuna: "These warriors are already killed by me. So don't hesitate! Fight! You shall conquer your adversaries in the ecstasy of battle." In Christianity there is Constantine's watershed dream before battle, usually rendered in Latin as *in hoc signo vinces*: 'in this sign, conquer'. The sacrament of Confirmation renders one a Soldier of Christ. All patriarchal cultures, for better and worse, conflate the initiatory and the bellicose, internal and external striving. Evidence of inner struggle by Constantine is scanty, however.

26 Muna Al-Awan, "Reading Shakespeare Cross-Culturally: An Islamic Approach."

Al-Awan quotes the famous Friar Lawrence speech from *Romeo and Juliet* for illustration of the dichotomy we've been exploring:

> Two such opposed kings encamp them still
> In man as well as herbs—grace and rude will;
> And where the worser is predominant,
> Full soon the canker death eats up the plant. (2.3.25-30)
>
> It is the conflict between "grace", the spiritual part of man, and "rude will", the animal part, that constitutes the tragic pattern of these plays. It is actually the battle between reason and passion. (95)

This jibes with the litany of references in *Hamlet* to the virtues of reason demonstrated earlier. Except for one thing: if reason is the spiritual part of man, it actually prevents Hamlet from meting his appointed vengeance. According to the play, his 'rude' passion is what is needed to accomplish what Lings is calling his spiritual ascent of the mysteries, vengeance as holy inner warfare.

Looking at Friar Lawrence's verses just before the ones cited above, there is a hint of a way through this apparent contradiction.

> Virtue itself turns vice, being misapplied,
> And vice's sometimes by action dignified.
> Within the rind of this weak flower
> Poison hath residence, and medicine power;

Reason is not a virtue in and of itself. 'Misapplied', that is, in Hamlet's case, over-thinking results in inaction: "And thus the native hue of resolution/Is sicklied o'er with the pale cast of thought." (III.1.84) The question remains as to whether the 'vice', the passion of vengeance, is 'by action dignified', thus in Ling's reading the apotheosis of action nearing the mysteries.

Because either way, 'canker death' awaits the protagonists.

The relevance of the four levels of interpretation still hovers, here. The delineations are not so neatly carved. Even Dante mentions that all but the literal are some form of allegorical. Critics have explored allegories galore—is Ophelia Grace personified?; is Gertrude 'Eve'?; is Claudius 'Satan'?; is Fortinbras 'lawlessness' or 'cosmos restored'?—and they all require a manipulation. They require an abeyance of aspects contradictory in the play itself; they require interpretation of the play's many ellipses; and they require meta-knowledge of texts or esoteric groups for a 'real' and full apprehension. After exploring the Christian ethical interpretation of Joseph Milne juxtaposed with Martin Ling's extolment of spiritual vengeance, there's precious little in the way of possible discourse between them. Are we doomed to wander interpretive purgatory?

We have to remember that this is poetry, a play, not a studied text. The great 'unplucked mystery' of this play may not be unearthed exegetically, but experientially. *Hamlet* lives on the stage, not the page. Not only the stage, but the sensorium within and without each person in the audience, from the penny payers on the gritty floor to the patrons on doughy cushions in the royal box. *Hamlet* inhabits each of them. The magic of this play manifests in that all of these possibilities are not only true, but *real*. The sorting of these possibilities is the business of life.

A last excursion-within-excursion: this time to ancient Greece, around the time the original tragedies birthing western culture were written, centuries before Aristotle's rationalism nearly codified them to death. In what is now Sicily, a mystic philosopher and sorcerer lived whose writings on the four elements became the basis of all western science. In those days, everything, including philosophy, was written in poetry—something that greatly annoyed Aristotle—and in the fragments of Empedocles' surviving poetry his vision of the cosmic movement of coming together and drifting apart is clear. Whether this cosmic inbreathing and exhalation is spoken of from the perspective of the individual elements being coerced into forgetful admixture, then released to return to separateness of their own volition; or the perspective of the *daimon,* or divine soul,[27] that forgets its divinity in coming into this world, only to return in remembrance, what drives this movement is the same. Love unites, strife moves things apart. They are both deities; they are both divine.[28]

There is a danger in not understanding that love binds us into forgetfulness, and it is strife that releases us, and that both are necessary, and both are divine movements. In the end of this little journey, understanding this might be helpful in our own experience of this play with full attention. While it is the love of Joseph Milne's reading of *Hamlet* that will bring events together into a sacred harmony, equally important is the strife of Martin Ling's reading to cut the cords of illusion initiating a return to sacred source. The mystery of *Hamlet* is the movement of Life. They are the Edenic fall and return as eternal and simultaneous.

Return

Arjuna and Hamlet are still in crisis, still playing out karma on various levels: personal, societal, cosmic. This burden manifests physically.

Hamlet creates himself through his own language. He talks himself into frequent vacillations—between resounding affirmation of his duty and elaborate game-playing in avoidance of it, between a fiery temper and cold dispassionateness, between passion and reason. He spontaneously fashions various enterprises during the play. Hamlet pretends to don an "antic disposition" to deflect attention from his real purpose—that of killing King Claudius—but his appearance to Ophelia after her father bans her from discourse with him shows him to be more than a little affected. She describes a telling encounter to her father.

27 *Daimon*, of course, gets turned from its divine meaning into the word 'demon' by early Christian 'thinkers'.

28 Peter Kingsley, *Reality*, 349-370.

My lord, as I was sewing in my closet,
Lord Hamlet, with his doublet all unbraced,
No hat upon his head, his stockings fouled,
Ungartered, and down-gyved to his ankle;
Pale as his shirt, his knees knocking each
other (II.1.86-90)

Here again is the wonder of the playwright's ambiguity. Is Hamlet truly affected by what is now a doomed love for Ophelia, and crumbles before her very eyes? Or is this mere play-acting to a purpose? If so, we are faced with a very cruel Hamlet toying with Ophelia's very real affections for him in order to reinforce his madness narrative. Yet, interior and exterior often reflect each other in Shakespeare, and nothing indicates that Hamlet has any real plan. His only instance of proactivity is organizing the play-within-the-play; other than that he is more buffeted than buffeting, and his trembling before Ophelia could be actual.

Compare that with Arjuna's quaking reaction to his crisis.

My limbs are rubbery, my mouth dries up,
my body quivers, and my hair bristles forth.
My bow Gandiva slips from my hand;
my skin burns. Unable to stand,
my mind rambles. (1.29-30)

Arjuna is the greatest archer alive; when his bow slips he is completely severed, not only from the task he must perform, but from who he is. Hamlet is similarly shaken during the encounter with Ophelia.

He raised a sigh so piteous and profound
As it did seem to shatter all his bulk
And end his being. (II.1.105-8)

Both Hamlet and Arjuna forget their original purpose and

the ground of being which necessitates it, and are forced to face their ineffectual individuality. Their crises stem from a particularized view of the world which sets it 'out there' in opposition to themselves and their desires and aversions. They see themselves as 'doers' of a repulsive action. In a very telling moment Hamlet cries, "The time is out of joint. O cursed spite that ever I was born to set it right!" He sets himself apart from his background, and also seems strangely proud of his destiny. His sense of selfhood is aggrandized by the magnitude of the task of setting the kingdom in order, while simultaneously crushed by its gravity.

Arjuna is similarly stuck on the notion that it is *he* who is the agent of his activity, and this obsession becomes the weight of his despair.

> I foresee misfortune in slaying my own kin in war. (1.31)

> I do not desire to kill those who are about to do the killing. (1.35)

> Surely it would be better to eat the the food of beggars in this world
> Than to have killed these mighty teachers.
> For having killed then, though they desire worldly gain,
> I should enjoy only blood-smeared pleasures here in this world. (2.5)

Both Hamlet and Arjuna presuppose their individual selfhood as agency of their action (karma), which posits an 'I' in confrontation with circumstance. This is our normal, habitualized view of experience, which leads to obstacles, crises, and suffering. Once this static viewpoint is overcome, crisis is ended. What needs to be done is the same, but the internal experience of the actor shifts dramatically.

Both men rely on rationalized thought to delay the inevitability of acting. Their reasoning is only valid within the limited context of their personal desire not to act in concordance with cultural dharma, that is, what they must do given their birth, deeds, and position in their cosmos. Early in the *Bhagavad Gītā*, Arjuna, envisioning certain cataclysmic outcomes of the immanent battle, comes to see them in terms of *adharma*, that is, not culturally and spiritually lawful. Thus ensues a rambling discourse on the destruction of family, caste-mixture, and fallen women that will suffer because *he* has to fight this battle. He has no inkling yet as to where the real battle lies.

An action not taken earlier in the *Mahābhārata*, at what is the fulcrum of the epic, calls into question even dharma itself. The Great War[29] begins in a shady dice game, where Arjuna's eldest brother, King Yudhiṣṭhira, son of the deity Dharma, gradually loses his entire kingdom, then his four brothers, then himself, and finally he loses the shared wife of all five brothers, Drāupadī. Yudhiṣṭhira's jealous cousins are drunk with the victory, and begin unwrapping his wife Drāupadī's sari before the entire court, dragging her mortified from the supposed safety of the red tent. Her four mighty husbands do nothing but watch, because the eldest Yudhiṣṭhira's word is law to them. He thinks he has given his word on these losing dice throws, and nothing can countermand his order. Even after Drāupadī, humiliated and degraded, pleads that her husband cannot have lost her after he has already lost himself to his cousins, the men continue to unwrap her. No one will break the word of the law, of what they consider unassailable *dharma*, to protect their wife and mother of their children.

They pull and pull and pull her sari, exhausted until they realize that Kṛṣṇa has performed a miracle against their lust by making her sari unwrap infinitely. She never forgets that her husbands chose the letter of the law over her honor. Later the question of literal versus actual dharma and action becomes murkier, especially with Kṛṣṇa's subsequent involvement in the

29 *Mahābhārata* translates as 'The Great War of the Bharatas'.

war. The point for now is that Arjuna has already been in a situation that demanded strong action and was confused and did nothing.

Hamlet has similar problems circumventing inertia and doing his culturally prescribed duty. He hears from the ghost of his father how he was murdered, and immediately interjects with:

> Haste me to know't that I, with wings as swift
> As meditation or the thoughts of love,
> May sweep to my revenge. (I.5.29-31)

In this moment of knowing, the proper course of action within Hamlet's Danish civilization spontaneously arises: he must kill the murderer of his father. Shakespeare's brilliance has the audience immediately feel this need for revenge, then frustrates it with the revelation that the murderer is now the king of Denmark, the one person whom Hamlet cannot just walk up to and justifiably kill. Even if he wanted to try the justice of the courts, ghosts make notoriously unreliable witnesses. Yet even within the framework of understanding this, Hamlet's I-centered perspective emerges as he refers to the urgent call to action as *my revenge,* as if he had been the one murdered. In full realization of whose name emblazons the theater marquee, the play *is* all about Hamlet.

When he slays meddlesome Polonius through the arras, it is a rare act of spontaneous behavior for Hamlet. Given the circumstance, this is actually one of the few times Hamlet acts within the realms of what Arjuna would call dharma during the play. Knowing the disgust he feels for his mother's marriage to the new king, Hamlet has no reason to believe that anyone but Claudius would hide himself in the queen's bedchamber. The thought of them together spurs Hamlet to act—as the first yelpings come from behind the arras, Hamlet draws his sword and slays the eavesdropper. No matter that Polonius and not Claudius hides there; given the vengeance structure, Hamlet's action is correct in that particular circumstance.

Does Hamlet really need to determine whether the ghost is genuine or an impostor? He believes that 'objective evidence' of the king's guilt will end the uncertainty—a doubt that doesn't exist when he first encounters the ghost—and enable him to act. Once again, Hamlet belies the direct knowledge that comes to him in the moment of his initial encounter with the apparition. He tells his best friend Horatio as soon as the ghost departs, "Touching this vision here, it is an honest ghost, that let me tell you" (I.5.154-5). Soon the rational need for 'rational' evidence supersedes intuitive insight gleaned through the moment, and Hamlet constructs an elaborate play-within-a-play in order to trap the king's conscience, and learn 'objectively' that which he—and the entire audience—already knows. The playwright juxtaposes reason and intuition, thought and heart, having each subtly undermine and then support each other. It is almost as if reason and thought are each vying for the attention of the audience, as they do within Hamlet:

> And thus the native hue of resolution/Is sicklied o're with the pale cast of thought, (III.1.84-5)
> That capability and godlike reason (IV.4.41)
> But thou wouldst not think how ill all's here about my heart, (V.2.188)

Without a teacher such as Kṛṣṇa, Hamlet is hard put to act from the point of view of what the *Bhagavad Gītā* terms discriminative knowledge (except, arguably, at the end of the play). He seizes upon whatever perceptions and sensations occupy his acute mercurial mind, toys with them, and becomes bounded by his speculative imagination. He has no vision of that which stands under and supports his world, and, living in the rotting state of Denmark, has little access to it.

This is where Kṛṣṇa serves his great purpose. He might tell Hamlet:

> There is no intuitive discrimination for one out of
> control,
> and for one out of control, no real perception,
> and without real perception, no peace.
> Where can there be happiness with no peace?
>
> When thoughts are guided by the wandering senses,
> understanding is carried away
> like wind carrying a boat on water. (2.66-67)

Kṛṣṇa must do for Arjuna what Hamlet cries out for when he says, "O that this too too solid flesh would melt, thaw, and resolve itself into a dew!" (I.2.135). His task, as is that of any teacher who embodies the teaching, is to free Arjuna from this limiting perspective, this view which breeds crisis and immobility. Kṛṣṇa realizes that a man cannot be wrenched from that which he clings to without severe damage; gradual steps and stages are necessary.

First Arjuna must realize how he has come to be immobilized.

> When a man dwells upon objects of sense,
> attachment to them is born.
> From attachment, desire is born,
> and from such desire anger arises.
> From anger arises delusion, and from delusion loss of
> memory;
> from loss of memory the destruction of intelligence,
> and from this destruction, he perishes. (2.62-3)

Here Kṛṣṇa schematizes the process by which one enters crisis. Anyone who has become angered due to conflicting desires and subsequently 'lost control' of him or herself, or of the situation, will recognize this progression. Kṛṣṇa wants Arjuna to watch this process, to discriminate between an 'I' attached to sense objects and that which generates both of these: the eternal absolute, bringing the moment into being.

Note that it is not sense objects themselves bringing on this declination, but the dwelling upon them hooking the attachment. Once on the battlefield Arjuna dwells—repeated thoughts or mental focus—on those with whom he must fight; instantaneously an 'I' arises, attached to them by opposition in circumstance. The desire takes form as either attraction or aversion to the sense objects; in this case, Arjuna wishes to avoid fighting against people he is attached to. But he forgets how he is attached to them in the first place, how all things are unified through a common ground, and is thus unable to discriminate between correct and incorrect action, between dharma and adharma. A human immobilized by crisis resides in hell.

The 'loss of memory' is more than forgetting what to do. The word in Sanskrit is *smṛti-vibhrama*, the 'wandering off of remembrance'. *Smṛti* is so important that it is one of the two categories encompassing all of Sanskrit literature. The other is śruti, literally 'heard', which describes the original revelation birthing Indian culture: the *Ṛgveda*, the *Āraṇyakas* and the *Upaniṣads*. These are aural/oral poems and writings going back many thousand of years. All of the subsequent texts, including epics such as the *Mahābhārata* and the *Rāmāyaṇa*, are considered *smṛti*, or recollection of this original vision. What has wandered is Arjuna's 'membering' of his body within the context of the wisdom of his culture.

And the body experienced through the vision of his culture includes much more than the anatomical definition westerners are accustomed to, and any understanding of unity and spiritual states relies on this difference. Kṛṣṇa speaks of this 'extended' body as the field (*kṣetra*), taking terminology from the Saṁkhya and Yoga philosophical systems:

The great elements,[30] the consciousness of 'I',[31]
intelligence[32] and the unmanifest,[33]
the eleven senses,[34]
the five realms of the senses,[35]
desire and aversion, pleasure and suffering,
the whole organism, consciousness, steadfastness:
this, briefly, is the field and its transformations.
(13.5-6)

The body here includes the elements and the senses; that is, the whole 'exterior out there' is really one with internal experience; your body includes what you sense: there is no separation. In fact, the first lines of the Gita are *dharma-kṣetre, kuru-kṣetre,* usually translated as 'the field of dharma, the field of the battle of the Kuru family'. The deeper layer here has the field meaning the full realm of experience, your *life,* wherein all the conflicts of dharma are played. The vision Kṛṣṇa prepares Arjuna for is radical unity, I and circumstance[36] melded into the one source from which both arise, the realization that there is no 'world out there'; there is only the sensation of your experience. This begs the question of the illusory nature of reality, looked at anon.

---

30 These are the traditional five elements of earth, water, fire, air and ether or space.

31 The term *ahamkāra* literally means 'I-maker', an integral aspect of experience. Without a sense of being in one place as opposed to another, it would be impossible to cross a room or navigate this world in any way. Not to be confused with *asmitā*, or I-ness or ego, which is the delusion that the sense of I is the doer of all activity, and thus considered a hinderance to direct knowledge.

32 The *buddhi* is the gateway between the divine and human, and the organ that makes experience of the divine realms possible. Other terms in other systems are Intellect or Imagination.

33 The ground of being, the divine feminine as pure *potentia*.

34 The eleven are the five organs of perception: eyes, ears, nose, skin and tongue; the five organs of action: hands, feet, mouth, anus and genitalia; and the mind.

35 Sound, touch, color, taste and smell.

36 From the under-read Spanish philosopher Ortega Y Gasset, in *Meditations on Quixote* (1914): "I am I plus my circumstance. If I do not save it, I do not save myself."

Because of his lack of realization, Arjuna is frozen facing this circumstance, which is his own life, which is *his own body*. His thoughts about where he is and what he has to do coalesce into a rigid self, and his ability to act congeals into reification—becomes a solid 'thing'—an intractable and infertile field yielding suffering as its fruit.

Like Arjuna, Hamlet suffers from immobility; he cannot seem to kill his uncle, although all winds blow in that direction. Unlike Arjuna's, however, his personal crisis is never fully resolved, and reoccurs throughout the play. He thinks himself into and out of action, and amazingly, sees the process as it happens.

> Thus conscience does make cowards of us all,
> and thus the native hue of resolution
> Is sicklied o'er with the pale cast of thought,
> And enterprises of great pith and moment
> With this regard their currents turn awry
> And lose the name of action. (III.1.91-6)

He tries to motivate himself through language ("O, from this time forth, my thoughts be bloody, or be nothing worth!"), but these are merely 'words, words, words'—verbiage spewn from passionate attachment to an ephemeral idea. He berates himself for this process, over which he has no control.

> Why, what an ass am I! This is most brave,
> That I, the son of a dear father murdered,
> Prompted to my revenge by heaven and hell,
> must (like a whore) unpack my heart with words
> And fall a-cursing like a very drab,
> A scullion! (II.2.591-5)

Arjuna, wants to know "what then impels a man who performs evil, unwillingly, driven as if by force?" Kṛṣṇa answers directly:

> This desire, this anger,
> originating from the *guṇa* (attribute) of passionate action (*rajas*),
> all-consuming and greatly evil (*papam*):
> understand this to be the enemy here.
> For just as the bearer of fire[37] is enveloped by smoke,
> and similarly a mirror by dust,[38] an embryo by the womb,
> so is this (intelligence/*buddhi*) concealed by that (passion). (3.37-8)

Most translators prefer to translate *papam* as 'sin', a word overburdened with Christian eschatology. For Kṛṣṇa *papam* ('evil') is not the abstract moral imperative of 'sin' that results in a putative future reward of eternal suffering or bliss. Hamlet is hamstrung by this *idea* when he sees Claudius kneeling and cannot do what he needs to to restore correct order, *dharma,* to the kingdom. Arjuna learns that evil and its reward happen in the moment of experience— that hell is 'evil' activity taking one further from liberation, and that 'good' deeds and thoughts bring one closer to it, or sustain life *as* heaven. And liberation is not *from* some thing, but instead, liberation *into* the grounding vision of the divine. Saturation not separation.

Arjuna cannot fathom the restraint necessary to overcome this compulsive desire that smothers wisdom. The mind "is turbulent, strong and hard. Its restraint, I think would be as difficult to accomplish as controlling the wind." Kṛṣṇa dispassionately repeats throughout the *Gītā* what is required for liberation:

---

37 The Vedic deity Agni who bears the prayers and oblations of the sacrifice to the gods; who comes close in later Yogic language to represent *buddhi*, the organ through which the divine and human realms connect.

38 The metaphor of coming to realize the divine by polishing the mirror of the self is especially beloved by Sufis.

> Abandoning entirely all desires
> originating in personal intention;
> having exercised complete restraint
> over all the senses by the mind;
> let one be stilled little by little,
> through understanding (*buddhi*) firmly grasped;
> and fixing one's mind in the Self.
> Do not think of anything. (6.24-5)

In order to help Arjuna recover his dharmic body, Kṛṣṇa describes the 'man of steady wisdom':

> When one leaves behind all desires of the mind, Arjuna,
> and is content in the self through the self,
> then, it is said, one's insight stands firm.
> One whose mind is not troubled amidst suffering,
> whose desire for pleasure has gone,
> whose passion, fear, and anger have departed,
> is said to be a sage of steady meditation.
> One who is dispassionate toward all things,
> and neither rejoices nor dislikes encountering the
> pleasant or unpleasant—
> that one's wisdom stands firm. (2.55-7)

This overlaps Hamlet's description of Horatio:

> For thou has been
> As one, in suff'ring all, that suffers nothing;
> A man that Fortune's buffets and rewards
> Hast ta'en with equal thanks; and blest are those
> Whose blood and judgement are so well comeddled
> That they are not a pipe for Fortune's finger
> To sound what stop she please. Give me that man
> That is not passion's slave, and I will wear him
> In my heart's core, ay, in my heart of hearts,
> As I do thee. (III.2.66-75)

This leads down a skip-road regarding Fortune. The 'being played like a flute' analogy recurs later in the very same scene, where Hamlet, in the exultant throes of having Claudius reveal his regicidal self by departing the play-within-a-play 'marvelous distempered', challenges Guildenstern to play a pipe. Guildenstern, fully in the Claudius camp as a spy, is still trying to extract from Hamlet the cause of his wit's end. He can neither play the flute nor Hamlet, who replies with a juicy double-entendre: "S'blood, do you think I am easier to be played on than a pipe? Call me what instrument you will, though you can fret me, you cannot play upon me." (III.2.336-8) Hamlet then proceeds to show how it is done, playing Polonius like a downmarket viol by having him parrot successive cloud shapes that he pretends to see. And they are indoors. That Polonius is in essence a spying, overinflated fool with no real inner qualities helps to undercut what sympathies the audience might have for him when he is slain in the next scene.

In Hamlet's Christian world the divine feminine is denigrated but not yet fully marginalized. Fortune, or Fortuna, was once a goddess. Her wheel was throughout the medieval era a moral compass, but for later Renaissance England she became random and capricious.[39] In the sexual repartee between Hamlet and Rosencrantz and Guildenstern when they first meet, she is a 'strumpet'. This is echoed when Hamlet requests a player entering Elsinore to recite a speech referring to Priam's slaughter, foreshadowing the king's downfall:

> Out, out, thou strumpet, Fortune! All you gods,
> In general synod take away her power,
> Break all the spokes and fellies from her wheel,
> And bowl the round nave down the hill of heaven
> As low as to the fiends. (II.2.454-8)

These speeches project upon Fortune blame for the fall, and victimhood for all actors.

---

39 The contemporary group Dead Can Dance, on their cd *Aion*, penned a neo-Renaissance song entitled "Fortune Presents Gifts Not According to the Book."

> Whether it is nobler *in the mind* to suffer
> The slings and arrows of outrageous for-
> tune (III.1.57-8)
>
> What have you, my good friends,
> deserved at the hands of Fortune, that she sends you
> to prison hither? (II.2.233-4)

Not to put too much of a misogynist overlay here: yet even though there is an acknowledgement of fortune having some influence in positive outcomes, certainly here the play emphasizes and blames any downturn on Fortune personified as not a goddess, but a wonton trollop. It seems a very convenient way to keep God the Father blame-free for the vicissitudes of the turn of events.

Here, yet again, we are presented with the 'blood and judgement', or passion, versus reason dichotomy, with Fortune seeming to enjoy passion. Fortinbras, whose hot-headedness equals Laertes', but played out on a larger scale, begins the play in lawless pursuit of vengeance, battles off stage for a worthless piece of ground in the middle, and shows up at the end the beneficiary of Fortune. In the aftermath of the final scene, Fortinbras, arriving from the outside, has the 'dying voice' of Hamlet's vote for election to the monarchy of Denmark. Fortinbras says, "For me, with sorrow I embrace my fortune." (V.2.367)

Still, even noble Horatio falls prey to passion in the final scene as he attempts to follow Hamlet in death, reaching for the dregs of the poisoned wine. Hamlet denies him, maybe realizing that Horatio is the only person who knows the entire tragic story, and suited to tell it.

Although Horatio has loyal qualities, he functions more as a sounding board for Hamlet than a man of wisdom. Where then, in Denmark, can Hamlet turn to for understanding? The *Gītā* seems to be saying that this is not possible without a teacher, without someone who embodies a living tradition of wisdom. Kṛṣṇa is an avatar, a divine incarnation of Viṣṇu. So the teacher is ultimately the divine, the holy animating all life.

Kṛṣṇa and Arjuna 19th century folio.

Kṛṣṇa spends chapters two through ten of the *Gītā* explaining various aspects, or paths of liberation. Meditation, knowledge, renunciation of actions, wisdom and understanding—these are but worldly facets of an unexplainable, eternal, imperishable vision of what life *is*, one that Arjuna is ready for by the epiphany in chapter eleven. Kṛṣṇa loosens Arjuna's attachment to sense objects, and exhausts his desire for detailed knowledge *of*. With the words "I give you a divine eye," Arjuna's vision begins, a terrifying ecstasy of the entire world of experience collapsing *as his body*: "The worlds tremble, and so do I." He is brought to his knees by this vision of Kṛṣṇa as the ground of cosmic manifestation. Arjuna calls out:

> You are to be known as the supreme imperishable,
> the ultimate resting place of the All;

> You are the relentless protector of timeless *dharma*,
> the primeval *puruṣa* (pure consciousness).
> Thus is my understanding.
> I behold you who are without beginning, middle or end;
> of boundless power, with uncountable arms.
> The moon and sun are your eyes;
> your blazing mouth consumes the sacrifice,
> your radiance illuminates the entire cosmos.
> This space between heaven and earth,
> is pervaded by you alone in every direction. (11.18-20)

Arjuna kinesthetically feels the world—him as a self, the arrayed warriors, even the whole battlefield dissolving into the unmanifest. *I* and *that* as points of reference have disappeared. "I know not the directions of the sky and I find no refuge." His *I*, his ego, is shown to be the fiction that it is: it has nothing to do with anything when the whole cosmos is continuously being reabsorbed into the divine ground. Who then is the doer? Kṛṣṇa divulges his own nature:

> I am Time, the cosmos-destroyer,
> arising here to annihilate the worlds.
> Even without you, all the warriors arrayed in
> opposition will cease to be.
> Therefore stand up! Attain glory!
> Having conquered enemies,
> enjoy a prosperous kingship.
> By me they are already slain.
> Arjuna, you are merely the occasion. (11.32-33)

Arjuna is thus led to the ego-shattering experience of being the occasion for the manifestation of the world, with his ever-vacillating 'I' as only a referential construction. The ego is not the true self, does not endure beyond being a momentary point of reference obliterated in the timeless vision of Kṛṣṇa.

Kṛṣṇa appears to Arjuna as Viṣṇu Vishvarupa ('all-forms') in an 18th century Indian miniature.

Arjuna cannot last long in this vision of limitless possibility. It will be impossible to move until he experiences a body in the world. How could you move across a room unless to some extent you experience a self in particular space? This is not possible in a complete unitive vision. Arjuna has seen how the world comes into being, is held together, and resolves back into its source. The difficulty will now be incorporating this vision into the activity of living. During the rest of the *Gītā*, Kṛṣṇa makes this possible by providing Arjuna with a model of the world concordant with this vision.

Arjuna gains a new body, one that is fluid in circumstance, one that *is* fluid circumstance. His sense of 'I' no longer opposes the world, but is integral to a 'field', the battlefield, the field of *dharma*. He sees the One in the Many and the Many in the One.

At the close of the *Gītā*, Kṛṣṇa tells Arjuna, "Having reflected fully on this, do as you desire." His desire is fully aligned with *dharma,* he has "gained remembrance (*smṛti*)". He has recollected or uncovered the reality of the primal source, the ground and repository of all human possibility. Only now may he do as *he* pleases, because *he* has expanded beyond his fictitious fear-ridden ego to include his entire divine sensorium, and the entire past and ground of his culture. When he acts, he holds the whole cosmos together (*lokasamgraha*).

Does Hamlet's dark and muddied Denmark provide a method for obtaining the vision made possible through Kṛṣṇa? It certainly seems that he has gleaned and incorporated some knowledge by the end of the play. The near-death encounter with the pirates along with the discovery of the king's execution order have jolted him out of his self-referential world. There are two indications of this. One is his compassionate and apologetic attitude toward Laertes, first mentioned to Horatio:

> But I am very sorry, good Horatio,
> That to Laertes I forgot myself:
> For by the image of my cause I see
> The portraiture of his. (V.2.82-5)

Hamlet, in killing Leartes' father Polonius, has put Laertes in the same position of having to avenge a murder. It takes all of Claudius' guile to prevent a rebellion. Hamlet is sobered by the realization of the dire consequences of his activity. Even so, Hamlet's apology to Laertes before the swordplay caries a tone of condescension.

> Was't Hamlet wronged Laertes? Never Hamlet.
> If Hamlet from himself be ta'en away,
> And when he's not himself does wrong Laertes,
> Then Hamlet does it not, Hamlet denies it.
> Who does it, then? His madness. (V.2.234-8)

This is not the same elimination of agency that Kṛṣṇa advocates in the *Gītā*. Hamlet merely bifurcates his being so that one aspect shoulders the blame for another.

Still, the Hamlet of the final scene has for the most part forsaken personal ambition and desire, and is able to act within his own *dharma*, albeit too late to alter the tragic outcome. This is how he responds to Horatio's misgivings about the fencing match:

> Not a whit, we defy augry; there's a special
> providence in the fall of a sparrow. If it be now,
> 'tis not to come; if it be not to come, it will be now; if it
> be not now, yet it will come: the readiness is
> all. (V.2.218-21)

Kṛṣṇa says to Arjuna: "Treating pleasure and pain, gain and loss, victory and defeat as all alike, become *readied* for battle." In a readied state one is aware of all possibilities and attached to none, not even the outcome.

The battle described in the *Gītā* ends in horrible carnage. Hamlet ends with the stage littered with dead Danish royalty. How are they different? With his last breath, Hamlet orders Horatio to "absent thee from felicity"—that is, don't avoid future suffering by taking the 'easier' route of suicide—"and in this harsh world draw thy breath in pain, to tell my story." The legacy of pain and despair is incarnated in Horatio and tragedy is doomed to repetition. Whether Shakespeare intended to show it or not, the tragedy of Hamlet is the depiction of western man without a grounding vision from which to act.

The *Bhagavad Gītā* ends quite differently. Saṁjaya, who is telling the story to the blind King Dhṛtarāṣṭa, says:

> O King, each time I recall this marvelous holy dialogue
> of Kṛṣṇa and Arjuna,
> I rejoice again and again.
> And continuously remembering the awe inspiring
> form of Kṛṣṇa,
> My wonder is great and I rejoice again and
> again. (18.76-7)

Thus the story is the vision, to be recalled and lived through, moment to moment.

Stay, illusion!

Throughout ancient, and persisting in some of contemporary India, *māyā* is the illusory nature of reality, as well as the power of that illusion,[40] and considered a living deity. The modern consensus encompasses the range of more or less illusory and correct views of reality—depending on the various cable news show dictates—but this is not so. It is reality itself that is the illusion, and there is no real world 'out there' existing apart from the illusion. There is only *māyā*. 'All the world's a stage'; 'Life's a walking shadow'.

In the *Mahābhārata*, one story seeds the animosity between the two families and makes war inevitable. Arjuna helps the trapped deity Maya, rescuing him from a burning forest, and wins a boon from him. Arjuna asks Maya to create the palace of palaces for his brother and king of kings Yudhiṣṭhira, which he does. Not only does it gleam brighter than the sun, it also manifests whatever one thinks. Yudhiṣṭhira and Arjuna invite their cousin Duryodhana—whose name means 'dirty fighter'—to this palace. He is king of the rival half of the Bhārata clan,

40 *Śakti* is the female aspect of that power, flowing through the central column of the body, and *lila* is that same power of manifestation and illusion, seen as divine play, or in the case of *Hamlet*, a play.

and eventual leader of the army they will face. They neglect to mention the palace's peculiar features. In an episode out of a Buster Keaton slapstick, Duryodhana slips into an unseen fountain, opens a door and crushes his nose on an invisible wall, and rolls down an imperceptible staircase into a cistern. Yudhiṣṭhira, Arjuna, their brothers, and their wife Drāupadī all howl with glee at their miserable cousin's mishaps.[41]

From the mystic perspective, there is no question that the cosmos is an illusion. The only question left, then, is one of navigation. And navigational facility comes through knowledge of *māyā*.

What is not *māyā* is not of this world. Kṛṣṇa teaches:

> Īśvara (highest vision, lord, pure consciousness)
> abides
> in the heart center of all beings, Arjuna,
> through *māyā* causing all beings to move,
> attached to a machine (*yantra*). (18.61)
>
> Truly divine is *māyā*,
> composed of the *guṇas*[42] through me,
> and difficult to negotiate.
> Those who take refuge in me
> penetrate this *māyā*.

---

41 Duryodhana doesn't forget this indignity (not to mention breaching of the sacred guest-host relationship), and in vengeance destroys Yudhiṣṭhira and his brothers' kingdom in the aforementioned dice game. And Drāupadī never forgets her humiliation and attempted public rape by Duryodhana and his kin after the dice game, while her husbands just watch, adhering to the letter of dharma.

42 The three *guṇas* are an integral aspect of Yoga philosophy, and can only be lightly sketched here. They divide all of experience into *sattva* (light, wisdom, purity, peace), *rajas* (activity, passion) and *tamas* (indolence, density, ignorance). They are all apparent in every experience, in differing degrees. Although the tendency is to extol the virtues of *sattva*, you need *rajas*' energy to simply move, and cannot hammer in a nail without the density of *tamas*. The goal for the Yoga practitioner is to see life, experience, through the movement of these *guṇas*, which helps to remove egoic agency from life's activity.

During the long flexuous course of the *Mahābhārata*, one's literal word often becomes reified into law or dharma. This engenders many a doing and undoing. With the illusion of *māyā* endemic to reality, holding to verbatim speech provides at least some structure to tread upon. When, for example, Arjuna 'wins' a wife[43] in a contest amongst princes, he returns home and calls to his mother Kuntī, "Mother, look what I have brought home!" She replies, without looking, "You know you must share everything with your brothers." Thus Drāupadī weds all five brothers due to a seemingly offhand remark, spending equal time with each of them, and somehow regaining her virginity anew every shift.

Yet it is the cosmic deity Kṛṣṇa himself who twists the literal word and employs *māyā* to help Arjuna and his brothers win their war. Arjuna swears to kill Jayadratha, in vengeance for killing his son, by nightfall. Jayadratha hides, knowing sunset will invalidate Arjuna's vow. Kṛṣṇa then places his discus over the sun, darkly tricking Jayadratha into coming out of hiding. Meanwhile, Jayadratha's father sits in meditation with another vow: whoever causes *his* son's head to fall will perish. Thus Arjuna is trapped between fulfilling his vow, and dying if he does so. Omniscient Kṛṣṇa overhears this vow, and directs Arjuna accordingly. Thinking nightfall has come, Jayadratha emerges confidently from concealment. Not only does Arjuna instantly decapitate him with a rain of arrows, but those arrows carry his head directly into his father's meditative lap. He jumps up, thus causing his own son's head to fall to the ground. The father also perishes, receiving the brunt of his own curse, and no one has broken his word.

The most notorious example of keeping technically to the letter of speech occurs as Arjuna fights Droṇa, his invincible

43 Although there were contests amongst princes held to determine eligibility for husbandhood, most often the bride had the final say. For a particularly great woman—for example Sita, an incarnation of the Earth goddess—the gods themselves would participate in disguise. You could always tell them by their hovering about six inches above the ground.

teacher. Droṇa cannot be defeated unless he puts down his arms willingly. This he will only do in grief, if he learns that his son, Aśvatthāman, is slain. Kṛṣṇa then directs King Yudhiṣṭhira to name a random elephant 'Aśvatthāman', and have it killed. Rumors spread that 'Aśvatthāman' is dead. Droṇa, informed of 'Aśvatthāman's' death, seeks confirmation of this straight from Yudhiṣṭhira, who, as a son of the deity Dharma, never lies. Well, just this once, sort of. Yudhiṣṭhira says to Droṇa, "Yes, Aśvatthāman (the elephant) is Dead," mumbling the part crucial to Droṇa, who lays down his arms and is promptly decapitated. In his defense, remember that Yudhiṣṭhira 'lies' at the behest of a deity, Kṛṣṇa.

Do these examples, and others like them, reveal these unassailable heroes as less than honorable? Is Kṛṣṇa acting outside of dharma in order to save dharma? A broad overview of the epic might help here. It turns out that this is a purgative war requested by the Divine Mother herself. Humans have become petty, bellicose, and comprehensively adharmic. She tires of propping them up. She asks the gods for relief of this burden of carrying humanity. Kṛṣṇa, an avatar of Viṣṇu—*avatāra* literally means 'to cross down'—has an overall intent to guide the light of dharma from the age (*yuga*) that this war is the denouement of, to live through to whatever the next age engenders.

> In reality, whenever dharma decreases, Arjuna,
> and adharma emerges,
> then I send forth myself.
> For the preservation of the good
> and the destruction of evil,
> I come into being from *yuga* to *yuga*
> to establish dharma.

'Good' and 'evil' ambiguous acts are dwarfed in the eons of cyclic time. Kṛṣṇa plays more of a trickster character than normally considered, and calls to mind a cynical line from another of Shakespeare's tragedies, *King Lear*: "As flies to wanton boys are we to th' gods, they kill us for their sport," (IV.1.36-7) as well as Hamlet's softer "There's a divinity that shapes our ends,/Rough-hew them as we will" (V.2.10-11). This sort of fatalism in the face of tragedy is understandable in the west, in Shakespeare's—and our—time when human-generated carnage dominates the informational landscape. The *Bhagavad Gītā*'s remedy involves knowing deep cycles of civilizations rising and returning to their origin.[44] In spite of Shakespeare and the *Gītā* illustrating so many similar themes, it is the humanism of *Hamlet* that both draws us to empathic connection and limits its cosmic perspective. Hamlet is flawed humanity; Arjuna is deity forgotten. In reading the *Gītā*, this discussion of vast ages and illusory nature of reality all emanating from a disaffected deity abstracts one from the human drama on the battlefield and the dire need to work toward wisdom, knowledge of reality, and what that means for us as intersections of the human and divine. Our head is in the *Gītā*, our heart is with Hamlet, and in our hands rest decisions about our travels in these realms of crisis.

Kṛṣṇa offers a spiritual solution to crisis, and *Hamlet's* touches on the spiritual, but real apotheosis slides out of the prince's reach. Instead of the mystery of ages recycling, as in the *Mahābhārata* epic, *Hamlet* epitomizes the tragedy of violence as a solution itself—whatever its cleansing attributes—which reincarnates across generations. Still, within both shines a core teaching of doing what needs to be done to hold the cosmos together, without concern for personal fruition.

Divine Feminine

India has lost, or is about to lose, its mythic or imaginal dimension.[45] In the West our divine origins are dead and buried, a

---

44 As Plato understood in the *Timaeus*, relying upon his informants like Heraclitus, Empedocles and Parmenides.

45 As this is written, writers in India who challenge the fundamentalist Hindu ideology are being murdered, and rapes of young women in public escalate, all under the implicating silence of the current PM.

tombstone in a mall-encrusted graveyard with a weathered unreadable inscription as to who is even interred there. In India they can still read the inscription, and share these stories, albeit mostly in a cartoon or Bollywood format. But this only intensifies the unspeakable sadness of the degradation and assault of women going on there now, in one of the last places that embraces the Divine Feminine.

The *Mahābhārata* epic foreshadows all this. The attempted rape of Drāupadī in the aftermath of the dice game where her husband Yudhiṣṭhira, son of Dharma, loses his kingdom has already been detailed. Even though Kṛṣṇa, off stage, intervenes on her behalf, her abasement and humiliation remain unatoned for, hardly a consideration in the story. She exemplifies the experience of the Earth Mother in her dealings with petty tyrannical men and their destructive lusts. Eventually one of Drāupadī's husbands, Bhīma—not Arjuna—answers her call and eats the heart of the cheater of the dice game who called for her disrobing. But for the other combatants, issues related to the feminine are relegated to irrelevance.

Except one. One important storyline highlighting the feminine was prominent in the nine hour play *The Mahabharata*, directed by Peter Brook. After all this investigative analysis, it might be pleasant to just indulge in a story.

Like in *Hamlet*, proper kingship, lineage and transferral of power are central to the *Mahābhārata*. We begin with Bhīṣma, an invincible ageless warrior, son of a king and the river Ganges—a pretty good DNA combo. He is the only son in line for the throne, and embodies all the regal attributes imaginable. Instead of doing the usual—marrying to continue his lineage—he arranges a marriage for his lonely father with another king's daughter. This king agrees, only on the condition that the son of his daughter would inherit the throne over any children of Bhīṣma. Bhīṣma gives his word that if he marries, his children will not inherit the kingdom. The king says, "Yes, I trust you Bhīṣma, but what about your potential children?" He wants certainty in this deal. Bhīṣma solves the problem by taking an unalterable vow of lifelong continence. Although this vow for some reason causes great joy in the celestial realms—celebratory fireworks light up the skies—it births havoc in the world. The marriage is consummated, and likely because he is old, Bhīṣma's father sires a weakling son, Vicitravīrya—whose name ironically means 'unusually powerful'—and soon dies. This son, when grown, is incapable of 'winning' brides for himself, thus the lineage is threatened. So arrowproof Bhīṣma, in a trial of arms, wins three musically-named sisters for his feeble half brother: Aṁbā, Aṁbikā, and Aṁbalikā.

The second two sisters, Aṁbikā and Aṁbalikā, dutifully marry impuissant Vicitravīrya, who proves impotent, and soon, he too exits the world. Bhīṣma's vow and the dead king now prevent any future siring for the throne. Who can save the lineage? In an almost post-modern plot device, the poet composing the epic, the sadhu Vyasa, inserts himself into his own poem to impregnate Aṁbikā and Aṁbalikā. He is apparently in some kind of hurry, because he shows up at the pristine palace as an unwashed, ill-odorous mendicant. Aṁbikā turns white at the sight of Vyasa, and gives birth to Pāṇḍu the Pale, the 'father' of Arjuna and his brothers. Aṁbalikā averts her eyes when it is her turn to be impregnated, and her son is born blind: Dhṛtarāṣṭra, who eventually sires the hundred sons whose questionable behavior makes the great war fated. Thus both sides of this epic conflict form from the seed of the poet dictating the tale to the god Ganesha. Notice here, the queens are relegated to birthing more warriors for the fray and then essentially forgotten.

Their eldest sister, Aṁbā, is of a different ilk. Countering her sisters, she refuses marriage to Vicitravīrya, invoking her rights of the *svayaṁvara*, where the princess bride has her 'own choice' among the contestants. Bhīṣma gives her leave to return to her love, Śālva, but he roughly refuses her, calling her 'Bhīṣma's property'. Aṁbā has no choice but to return to Bhīṣma. She begs Bhīṣma to marry her, since he caused the whole mess by not following his destiny into kingship, and intervening when convenient by 'winning' wives for his father and brother. Still, Bhīṣma holds to his vow to have no intercourse with the feminine. Thus the woman who makes her own choice—embracing love—in this epic world is sentenced to be alone and rejected.

But Aṁbā invokes a formidable vow of her own: to bring down Bhīṣma whatever the cost. His rejection of the feminine—standing in concentrated maleness, without a partner, without progeny—is arguably the cause of all the destruction in the *Mahābhārata*. Aṁbā becomes a one-pointed arrow shredding the story with her unyielding intent. She becomes the anti-Bhīṣma. When the male world, that is, the warriors and princes, that she begs to champion her cause, fails in its courage to face Bhīṣma, she turns to a brāhman priest, an avatar of Viṣṇu. He at least fights Bhīṣma, though loses. She then practices extreme austerities in the Himalaya worshiping Śiva, Lord of Dissolution, with such focus and dedication that Śiva himself appears and grants her a boon. He allows that she will be reborn as a male to become an instrument in Bhīṣma's demise. Impatient, she lights an enormous pyre and dives in, hastening her rebirth as Śikhaṇḍin, son of one of the kings who had refused to champion her.

Thus, in this corrupt cosmos the feminine has to become masculine to defeat the greatest male warrior. Recognizing Śikhaṇḍin as the incarnation of Aṁbā, Bhīṣma refuses to engage with him-her because he sees him as a woman. Given a last chance, he refuses to connect with the feminine, even on his own terms on the masculine field of battle. He spends his last days pontificating, resting on a 'cushion' of arrows that Śikhaṇḍin and Arjuna shoot through him.

Balance rests upon the fulcrum of unity. Bhīṣma's abdication of his princely dharma at the outset of the *Mahābhārata* upsets any possible harmony of the male and female principles. Instead of holding the world together by begetting the next generation, he sires crisis after crisis, eventually Arjuna's as well. There is a saying from a commentary on the *Yoga Sūtras* that is likely quite ancient: "Ignorance is beginningless, but it does have an end." The end is the return to wisdom advocated by Kṛṣṇa, an inner knowing within which Arjuna still has a war to wage. This makes for a great story, and a violent cosmos. The search for the lost divine feminine brings us closer to the primal cause of crisis.

There are only two women in *Hamlet*. Starting with Gertrude, so much connects her with Genesis Eve. Psychoanalysis would either have us believe in an Oedipal relationship with her son Hamlet, or have the play read as some prurient Freudian dreamscape of Gertrude as wonton Eve, with her adulterous sexuality the weeded, fallen garden of Eden suffocating all but the serpent she aligns with. She takes the blame for the fall in the play, much the same as the Christian world blames Eve for the loss of paradise and the introduction of death. Methinks the psychoanalysts doth protest too much.

Certainly Shakespeare evokes echoes of Eden, especially the slaying of Cain by Abel:

> O, my offence is rank, it smells to heaven;
> It hath the primal eldest curst upon't,
> A brother's murder! (III.3.36-8)

He conflates that original murder with the Edenic expulsion tale by having a serpent as the agent of King Hamlet's murder while dreaming in his own garden. In the biblical myth jealousy is the motive for fratricide, but strangely, there is no patent intent given for Claudius' in *Hamlet*. This then begs the question of what was Eve's motive in disobeying the directive of the Creator in Genesis—who is demoted to mere demiurge by the Gnostic Christians—not to eat of the fruit from the tree of good and evil. Often 'curiosity' frames Eve's motive, but this is limiting and demeaning from a sacred perspective. As the Talking Heads song goes, "Heaven is a place, a place where nothing ever happens." The divine feminine demands change, even from what appears perfect. The ancients all revered her as the agent of creation *and* destruction. Humans *had* to leave Eden: death was already there. They would have perished of static boredom, because stasis is living death. You can blame Eve for necessitating the expulsion from Eden, but you can't blame her for the subsequent murderous behavior of her sons.

And so with Gertrude. But Martin Lings rightly doesn't let her off easily.

> The Queen is not merely Hamlet's mother; she is his whole ancestral line going back to Eve herself; inasmuch as she is Eve, she represents, in general, the fallen human soul, especially in its passive aspect... According to the letter of the law, the Queen is altogether innocent of the murder of King Hamlet and indeed altogether ignorant of it. But the fact that she was willing to marry a monster of a man almost immediately after having been widowed of his opposite makes her eminently qualified to personify the initial guilt of fallen humanity...since the Fall, as we have seen, may be considered as a murder, to personify the fall is to personify its guilt in that respect also, which makes Gertrude an accomplice of Claudius. (22)

An ex post facto accomplice. If there is a divine right of kings as vice-regency of God on earth, there is a divine right of queens to embody the goddess. Eve's connection to her divine origin is buried by the male deity taking sole credit for all aspects of creation. The natural world, the fruited tree, is her path back to a wisdom denied her. Gertrude, as the widowed queen of King Hamlet, suppresses her regal qualities and embraces her dead husband's brother in fear, marrying his soul-deadening world. She redeems herself at the end of the play, promising to abjure Claudius' lechery, and sacrifices herself for her son by drinking the poisoned wine intended for Hamlet.[46] The divine feminine, what Arjuna would call *prakṛiti,* constantly sacrifices herself, moment to moment, to bring about what is next: each evanescent iteration her child.

Török Irma as Ophelia in 1901.

Finally, "How now Ophelia?" Her heart-rending story may be the real tragedy of *Hamlet*. She embodies feminine grace lost in that muscular world. And let us be clear that it is not a masculine qua masculine that promulgates the mess. The masculine has already lost its divine moorings to the point of impossibility of retrieval. Hence, taking their theurgic cue not from the risen Christos but from the vengeful Old Testament deity, all problems up through this day are solved with violence. Not the cleansing violence of the divine mother, but the infinitely perpetuated violence of the lost 'I am' ego of the father. This ego is the real insatiable hungry ghost, wandering a parched purgatory.

46 One wonders about this image of poisoned wine in a chalice resulting in a seemingly senseless sacrifice looking very much like an inverted mass. Given the religious troubles permeating Shakespeare's days, and his possible outlawed Catholic heritage, a mass ending in bloodshed rather than communion (the pearl tossed in the poisoned chalice is called 'an union') is an apt metaphor.

What chance does a soul built for love and beauty stand in such a sordid cosmos? Ophelia's love is spurned by Hamlet;[47] she is no better than bait for her father and Claudius to try to suss out Hamlet's designs, and a mirror for Hamlet to discern the schemes of Claudius. Too weak to stand for her love, she sways to everyone's will until she has lost everything—her father dead, her brother gone, and her love weeded over and forgotten. Even at her funeral, Laertes and Hamlet vie in her open grave, not in expressions of true love, but in proclamations of their aggrandized egos. Their love never even lived enough to deserve the tomb they lie in.

But in madness she finds her voice. Hamlet's madness is feigned, coy, manipulative, self-protective, even while operative in the main to achieve the goal of removing Claudius. Ophelia's is creative, liberating, truth-directed. In her dissolution from the world, beauty finally has 'commerce with honesty'. She finds her way through connection to wild nature at her rawest and realest: the divine feminine embodied classically in Artemis. She sings trenchant poetic songs of death as child's play. Most actresses play her with distracted tics and violent jerks, but there is a serenity in her surrender that rarely is performed.

She informs the court through the language of flowers, in a hopeless attempt to seed Elsinore with *something* from the world of nature. No one takes advantage of this opportunity for self-reflection in the form of flower language offered from her. She hands out flowers to certain characters (IV.5.172-9), but if there was an original stage direction, it is lost, so even here we are faced with ambiguity. What did she give to whom? There is some tradition, but it really depends on the director's interpretation. Further ambiguity comes from the differing interpretations of the flowers themselves.

"There's rosemary, that's for remembrance. Pray you, love, remember. And there is pansies, that's for thoughts."

47 His famous "Get thee to a nunnery!" equally meant 'whorehouse', but the next line, "Why wouldst thou be a breeder of sinners?" points to the monastic meaning.

Because of her brother Laertes' response—"A document in madness, thoughts and remembrance fitted"—the consensus is that she gives both flowers to him. One question is, who does *she* think she is giving the flowers to?

Previously she had been singing snippets of songs related to death and maidenhood. These could be thoughts for her dead father, and also echo the ghost of King Hamlet pleading to his son, "Remember me." Anyone imputing a deeper Platonic reference of knowledge as remembrance—the Greek word for truth, *aletheia*, means 'to not forget'—can point here. And recall, when Arjuna has fully embodied the wisdom of his culture at the end of the *Bhagavad Gītā*, he states, "I have gained remembrance." Foreshadowing her looming exit from the stage, she really could be referring to herself. To take it a step further into the context of this discussion, we are asked to remember the divine feminine, whose expression is love, about to abandon the world that has abandoned her.

There is an ancient tale that may or may not go back to Shakespeare's time.[48] Eve and Adam in Eden were watched over by two particular stars. The stars recognized the trouble brewing in paradise, and sent messengers with certain tokens, who arrived just as the archangel, sword lifted, was expelling the original couple into the land of darkness and longing, and was about to seal the portal. The angel blocked the messengers, until they raised their tokens, and one said, "I am the gift of the King of Silver Fishes, and I represent strength!" and the other said, "I am the gift of the Queen of the Golden Harvest, and I bring comfort!" The angel recognized his siblings and lowered his sword, allowing them to pass in the form of rosemary and lavender, strength and comfort. And they have continued to accompany humanity in this darkness, to show the path back home to the starry garden from which they originally came.

Here rosemary connects back to the fall from and return to Eden, so integral to the proceedings of *Hamlet*. It is given and

48 Taken from Alan Chadwick's *Performance in the Garden*, and Maria Geuter's *Herbs in Nutrition*.

worn at weddings and funerals, thus echoing the central cause of Hamlet's melancholy: "The funeral baked meats did coldly furnish forth the marriage tables" (I.2.181-2). Most risen in Ophelia's distracted mind are the funeral for her father, which should have been a huge state affair, but is downplayed by Claudius, and the wedding that she never gets with Hamlet. Pansies exemplify thoughts, faithfulness and grief. Likely she gives the rosemary to Laertes as a stand-in for Hamlet, to remember love, and the pansies to Laertes as himself for thoughts true to their father, and maybe even as flowers to place in the grave she will soon inhabit.

It may not be all that important whom Ophelia gives rosemary and pansies to, since they are mainly for the audience, to remember themselves.

"There's fennel for you, and columbines."

Because of the connection both flowers have with adultery, an argument for Ophelia handing them to either Claudius or Gertrude can be made. Columbine has an association with foolishness (its shape resembles a jester's crown) and deceived love, both of which apply more to Gertrude in her foolish and misguided attachment to Claudius. They also connect with cuckoldom and male adultery, so possibly they are for Claudius, whose wife, after her confrontation with Hamlet in the bedchamber scene, has left him for a more spiritual life.

Fennel is an emblem of flattery, the most salient quality of Ophelia's departed father Polonius, and according to Hamlet the sad direction towards which the Danish court heads, embodied in the verbiage of the courtier Osiric. These are more connected to Claudius and the Elsinore he creates. Fennel also casts out evil spirits, either in the murderous king himself, or those hovering over all of Denmark's dark rotten state. Like Claudius' rule, fennel wilts quickly, so is known for sorrow.

"There's rue for you, and here's some for me. We may call it herb of grace a Sundays. O, you must wear your rue with a difference."

If we give the previous flowers to the king, then rue is given to Queen Gertrude. Rue is a bitter herb whose main qualities are repentance and sorrow, and it was also used as an abortive. She shares rue with the queen: both are in sorrow, having lost love and family, though the repentance aspect applies more to Gertrude, who has married her brother-in-law and by now regrets it. Ophelia's is the rue of innocence, and Gertrude's is of experience, thus she wears it with a difference. Rue is called herb of grace o' Sundays, because one would dip it in holy water entering a church to obtain grace. Ophelia is opening them both up to the redemptive grace, associated with Mary, 'full of grace', the closest to the divine feminine as the church of that day gets. And most poignantly, it points to Ophelia aborting her own life by submerging herself in the waters.

"There's a daisy. I would give you some violets, but they withered all when my father died."

Quite possibly, the daisy, representing innocence, goes to no one. It also represents love's victims, so Ophelia could claim it, and possibly she does, just giving it a longing look. Violets belong to the faithful. Certainly her father is faithful to the malignant throne of Denmark, so his slaying by Hamlet ends all fidelity. It also echoes the mention of violets in Act One, back when we were all so innocent. Her brother Laertes chides her for giving audience to Hamlet and countenancing his love as abiding, saying, "Hold it a fashion and a toy in the blood,/A violet in the youth of primy nature" (I.3.6-7). What Ophelia sees as a garden of love, Laertes calls a youthful fling. Maybe Ophelia's love dies then and there. And maybe Laertes remembers and laments this reproach, as in the graveyard scene he hopes that "from her fair and unpolluted flesh/May violets spring!"

Shakespeare saves his most exquisite poetry for Queen Gertrude's portrayal of the death of Ophelia.

There is a willow grows askant the brook
That shows his hoar leaves in the glassy stream.
Therewith fantastic garlands did she make
Of crowflowers, nettles, daisies, and long purples
That liberal shepherds give a grosser name,
But our cold maids do dead men's fingers call them.
There on the pendent boughs her crownet weeds
Clamb'ring to hang, an envious sliver broke,
When down her weedy trophies and herself
Fell in the weeping brook. Her clothes spread wide,
And mermaid-like awhile they bore her up,
Which time she chanted snatches of old lauds,
As one incapable of her own distress,
Or like a creature native and indued
unto that element. But long it could not be
Till that her garments, heavy with their drink,
Pulled the poor wretch from her melodious lay
To muddy death. (IV.7.164-181)

How Gertrude comes upon this painstaking report is not accounted. One must imagine that she witnessed it, pulling this illustration out of the depths of her own soul, Ophelia's late power of voice having been somehow transferred to her.

Ophelia goes to a weeping willow—symbol of forsaken love and mourning—that hangs over a 'glassy' stream, which would make it slow-moving and deep. She devises garlands of four flowers, which have many associations. Crowflowers are either buttercups, or wild Williams, or Ragged-Robin, which grow in wetlands. Buttercups denote ingratitude and maidenhood, while wild Williams are considered beneficial to the heart. Here also Ophelia claims the daisy for herself, flower of innocence, easer of various pains, and curiously, steeped in wine to treat insanity. And with nettles one begins to wonder if this is a curative garland she weaves. Nettles generate heat (Roman soldiers stationed in Britain rubbed themselves with them to stay warm), are extremely nutritious, a great internal cleanser, and an antidote for poisons. Long purples are wild orchids, although another interpretation is purple foxglove, from whence the heart medicine digitalis comes: again, a heart reference. As for the wild orchids, the connection is with love, beauty and refinement, or finery, the floral adornment she weaves.

She climbs a downhanging branch with this crown garland, not for herself, but for the tree itself. The practice of hanging strips of cloth—'weed' has a double meaning of clothing or garment—upon a tree near a spring or water source is pre-ancient all over Britain. The tree—called a clootie tree—takes on the suffering of the supplicant. They are still in regular use. Ophelia may be offering her sorrows to the tree, but they are too much even for this willow, and the branch she stands upon breaks, dropping her into the 'weeping brook'. She floats for a while, singing bits of old hymns, not only in perfect serenity with what has happened, but "like a creature native and endued unto that element"; she essentially has become an undine or water nymph. She has already left the world and is returning to the elements from which she came, becoming one with them. Her peace comes from knowing her connection with divine Nature. Ophelia abandons the "rank and gross" "unweeded garden that grows to seed" (I.2.135-6), in order to seed love in the garden she came from.

"Ophelia" by Alexandre Cabanel, 1883.

Ophelia's passing is not a suicide, but a surrender. It is telling that charges of suicide come from a lost masculine authority incapable of understanding what she has done. The gravediggers ('clowns' for Shakespeare are rustics, used for low comedy) are the first to conclude she has killed herself, using twisted legal logic to justify her burial in sanctified ground ("How can that be, unless she drowned herself in her own defense"). The church performs 'maimed rites', finds her natural death 'doubtful', and does not deign to have the abrupt service performed by a priest, but by a Doctor of Divinity. She is at least allowed to wear a maiden's garland, though even her virginity is also mistrusted. Thus we have two very different understandings of Ophelia's death operative. One derives from the masculine bureaucracy: is sexual, rational, and saves face. The other, viewed through Gertrude, the only other woman in the play—at least for a short while—is poetic, loving, and concordant with nature. The preponderance of critical commentary favors suicide, or at least a madness-mitigated taking of her own life. There is even much discussion of Gertrude pushing Ophelia in. One really can't expect much more in a society lost and unbalanced, Elizabethan or contemporary.

Denouement

The great question streaming through this whole paper remains: is vengeance a viable spiritual path? Is it only then operative on a metaphoric level of the spiritual warrior slaying internal foes? Redemptive retribution can only be a reality in a masculine-dominated sphere. What may have once been a viable path for the warrior-princes in Arjuna's time, or a metaphoric path for princes and priests in Hamlet's Elizabethan world, or a theurgic path in traversing any world religion, has degraded fully in our day. In practice, violence is now the preferred—and often the only—venue for problem-solving. The frequency with which violence worldwide occurs in the name of religion speaks to the scope and depth of this true tragedy. Is there any reason to continue the farce that vengeance has a purifying spiritual aspect?

Yet there seems nothing else. War on Drugs, War on Cancer, War on Christmas, for Christ's sake: but never War on War. Always War on Peace. In the *Mahābhārata* war is inevitable, war is dharma, war is righteous, an opportunity to abnegate one's ego and self-agency within action *that ought to be done*. The *Bhagavad Gītā* offers the possibility of connection to the divine, but it still leads to epic death counts and the devastation of the very dharma it seeks to save. Similarly, one can excavate spiritual principles in *Hamlet* of atoning vengeance reestablishing some harmonic order, but really, all these songs play out in the key of death.

The divine feminine can be devastatingly destructive and violent. Just ask Durga or Kali. Hurricanes, before they were seeded, made more sense cosmologically when given female names. That is the natural violence of change, of Gaia maintaining and rebalancing her body in mysterious ways. Eating to live—whether vegan or carnivore—is impossible without violence. The goddess rules equally over life and death. And finally, the mystic—here embodying the divine masculine—bears witness to the ultimate destruction of the entire universe of experience, instant to instant, as in Arjuna's vision; which is staged macrocosmically as entire civilizations disappear and reemerge through the yugas. Including ours.

At the risk of being reductionist or trendy, and of forsaking Hamlet and Arjuna and their toils, we have belabored this examination of the lost divine feminine because all crisis is born of lost divinity in a culture, whether masculine, feminine, or more often, both. Yes, crisis, or strife, is necessary for any movement, from hunger for food to longing for the divine within. But crisis within a civilization unmoored from the numinous drifts only into continued incarnation of the same meltdown, merely played by different actors. The deepest tragedy of *Hamlet* is that nothing substantial changes. Maybe it is only a small solace that even though extinction follows the *Bhagavad Gītā*, there is revelation, light, and understanding within it.

In fact, all culture, even this lost western one, is originally born from the divine, always emerging from a connection between the holy and the human. The untempered lost masculine, especially in places of entrenched religious fundamentalism—Christian, Islamic, Hindu, Judaic, etc.—expresses itself in exaggeration of its own worst suppressive and violent qualities. Only an irredeemably astray society can cast those actions as 'moral'. You only suppress what you fear, and the ego is nothing if not fear itself.

And war, the masculine solution to everything, cannot restore it. It takes something far more virile. All that is left is the unqualified Gaiaic power of the divine feminine to completely cleanse through her impersonal destruction, and to start again, for us to root out the flickering flames of wisdom and clasp them within, just possibly to spark what is unimaginably next.

Connecting Earth to Heaven
Bhūmi-Svarga Prāṇāyāma

The Practice

We'll start with a straight explanation of the practice, and follow with some theory behind it. You can do this practice in any position, even lying down, but it seems seated with a relaxed, straight back is best. Either on the floor or in a chair.

Focus on the experience of your *sushumna* or central energetic column. It runs for most people from the perineum—where you sit—through the center of the body, just in front of the spine, to the top of the head. The seven chakras it connects begin at the level of the perineum; move to the level of the sexual organ; then to the navel; then to the heart; then to the bottom of the throat; then to a point between the eyebrows; and then to the crown of the head.

There are all sorts of exercises associated with the chakras ('wheels' so-named for the experience of energy there) but this is not really one of them. If it helps to increase your awareness of the central energetic pathway, you could chant the traditional seed sounds (*bīja*) at each of the chakras, in ascending order: *lam; vam; ram; yam; ham; aum*. The short 'a' sound in Sanskrit is more like a short 'u' in English, so 'lam' would sound like 'lum'. There is no sound for the crown chakra, as experience there is considered the unmanifest ground of being. In recent decades many people have devised variations on the seed sounds, but this is the most traditional one, and it correlates exactly with inner experience.

The practice of *bhūmi-svarga prāṇāyāma* is fairly simple, with two steps to help you get there. First, with your inhale, trace that inner column from your perineum up to your heart. If you are seated in a chair, try to expand the awareness of your seat to include your feet touching the ground, so that when you are inhaling, you are drawing up from the earth herself. With your exhale continue to trace the path up through the throat and third eye to the crown.

No need to force the breath, nothing strenuous, just very relaxed normal breathing. Then with the next inhale, follow the breath down from the crown through to the heart, and with the exhale, trace the breath back to the root chakra and the earth.

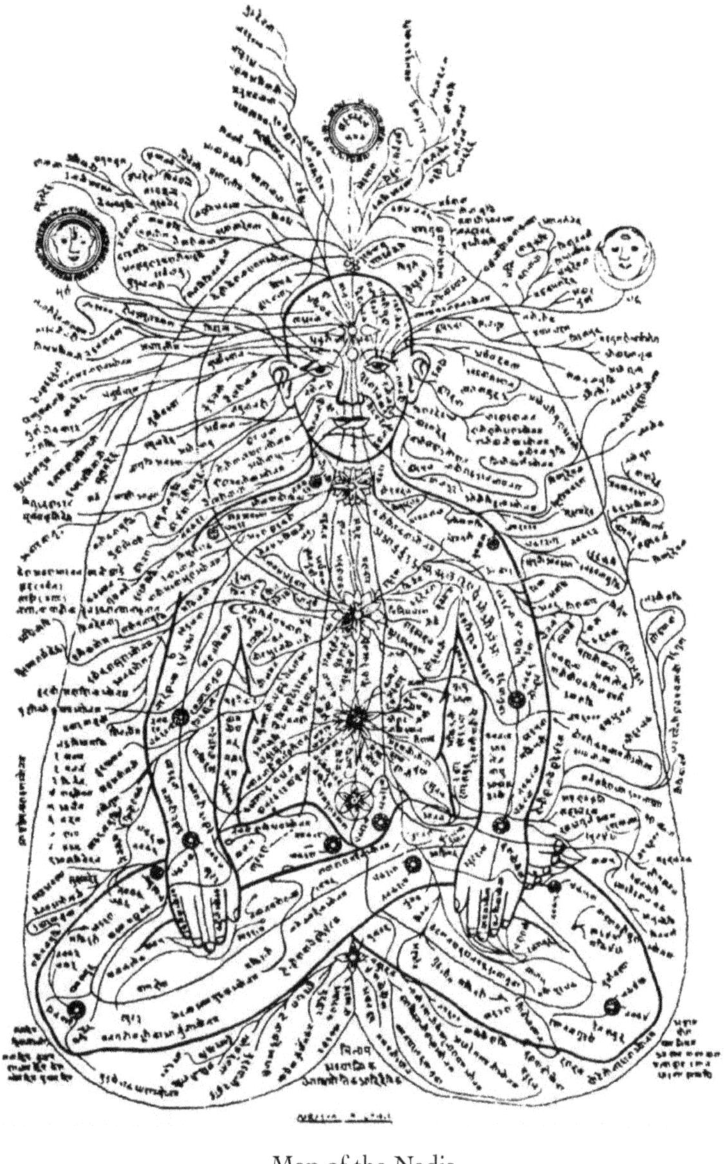

Map of the Nadis

After a few repetitions this should become fairly easy and natural. The next part takes a certain relaxed awareness. Instead of taking the inhale from just the root chakra, *simultaneously* trace breath from the root to the heart, *and* from the crown to the heart with the inhale. So both breaths, which are really one breath, meet in the heart. With the exhale, the breaths cross, as it were, and continue simultaneously from the heart to the crown and from the heart to the root/earth.

The 'trick' is how to be aware of your crown in heaven, your seat upon the earth, and the heart where they meld simultaneously. You cannot do this with mental focus, you can only do this by relaxing into the origin of awareness.

If for some reason the simultaneous connecting of earth and heaven to the heart through the breath is difficult, stick to the single movement outlined in the first part. There is no reason to struggle with any of this, and in fact struggle or forcing anything is not a good idea when working with subtle energies.

In fact, as with all *prāṇāyāma*, once you disappear into the practice (and you are no longer *practicing*, but there), you may notice a more subtle movement of *prāṇa*, *prāṇa* itself rather than its grosser manifestation, the breath. It is the breath within the breath.

If any of this feels wrong, or seems to have an adverse effect, stop immediately. If it is not for you, it is not for you. My hope is that this practice is of assistance in some way.

The Theory

First, something about the origin of the practice: take it for what it is. About five years ago this came to me in a deep meditation all at once, from whence I don't know. At the time, it was indicated that it was not just for me, but for public consumption. Still I did not tell anyone about it until I had done it myself. It has really taken until now for me to understand what the purpose of the *bhūmi-svarga prāṇāyāma* is. The word for earth in Vedic Sanskrit is *bhūmi*, and the word for heaven is *svarga*. They were experienced as deities in the life of the Vedic bards, as they still can be for us.

As always, you are welcome to take what I have to say with as many grains of Himalayan salt as you can palate. I am not a yoga instructor, I have no certificates, although I have taught Sanskrit, *prāṇāyāma* and meditation at certificate courses. I spent eleven years in the 80's and 90's studying in a very traditionally-oriented ashram on Long Island, Yoga Anand Ashram, founded by a woman from Calcutta, Gurani Añjali. As far as I know, there was no specific school involved: Guruma learned from her teacher, who learned from his, on and on back to Patañjali, if not in actuality, at least in transmission. The focus there was less upon the āsanas than upon the yoga tradition or *marga* itself, and we studied all the traditional eight limbs of yoga, the Sanskrit literature, and very smartly, Western philosophy, to understand the ground we don't realize we stand upon.

Unfortunately, a brief discussion of the basic presupposition of yoga is needed. Normally I wouldn't consider this necessary, but for an experience at a panel discussion not long ago. A young man who runs a yoga center, who apparently was well-versed in the *Yoga Sūtras*, got into a disagreement with another panelist about radical stillness as the spiritual ground. He claimed that there was no absolute stillness in yoga, and that all stillness is relative.

Yoga is a radical system, as radical as they come—apparently this is not well understood by some current practitioners, possibly because those running the training don't understand either. So let's go right to the definition (these translations are mine) of yoga at the beginning of the *Yoga Sūtras*:

yogaś citta-vṛtti-nirodhaḥ

or, Yoga is the cessation of swirling experience.

And what are these swirls or fluctuations (*vṛtti*)? They include sleep, memory, imagination, correct thought, and perception. It is the last one that shows how radical and absolute Yoga is. Even if there is still sense perception, then it is still not the definition of yoga. A *vṛtti* is any movement within. The cessation of *vṛtti* is absolute stillness. There isn't even a you to be not there.

In the pivotal chapter eleven of the *Bhagavad Gītā,* Arjuna, given a divine eye, has lost his mooring in the complete totality which is the body of Kṛṣṇa. How can he move anywhere if there are no directions, and no self to face a direction? He returns to his 'four-armed form' so that he can do his dharma on the battlefield. But is there a difference in having had this experience? Or are we doomed to being either lost in transcendence or lost in duality?

There is a hint in one of the Vedic poems, *Ṛgveda* 10.90, *The Puruṣa Sukta,* or "Hymn of the Cosmic Human." This poem describes how the cosmic being is sacrificed to become this world.

> From his navel the intermediate atmosphere arises;
> From his head the sky likewise moves;
> The Earth comes from his feet;
> And the directions from his ear:
> Thus the worlds are ordered.

We can look at this transformation a few ways. We can think of some original sacrifice of the divine to generate this world, a long time ago, and that there is a sacred origin to this world that we hope to participate in. And this is a wonderful thought.

Yet there is a deeper, more radical experience open to us. *You* are Puruṣa, and every time you take a step, the earth is created for you and through you. There is no other earth out there independent of your stepping on it. Anything you think is out there, a thing in itself, is just illusion (*māyā*), divine play (*līlā*). And it is so divinely wrought, that you have to realize your own divinity to recognize it. *The illusion is real.*

This is actually pretty scary stuff, but only scary to an ego that thinks it is a real, abiding separate entity. As divinity we are both the ground of stillness, and the manifestation from stillness, in oneness.

This gets us back to *bhūmi-svarga prāṇāyāma*. Not only does the earth come from your feet, but the sky, the heavens, from your head. This practice offers a connective between the heavens and the earth, and an opportunity to realize how they arise through us.

Hopefully this can be corrective of a possible imbalance. On one hand we have lost our real connection to the underground deities, the so-called dark goddesses like Kali and Persephone. When chthonic goddesses are unappreciated, things that are not so pleasant arise from the depths. We know what they are. Many people talk about worshipping Gaia or Demeter, but the connection has to be real, actual, powerful, and beyond thought to make any difference to her or us.

The tendency across various spiritual disciplines is to transcend, ascend, rapture out, move to the next dimension, be high. Not to mention the confusion of recreational drug use with spiritual experience. Kirtans bring bliss, but do they bring reality? (Not that I have anything against bliss.) My suspicion is that when the first Indian yogis met American and European students, they focused on practices that took them out of their bodies, because Westerners are so stuck in the physical, and needed to see that there is something else.

Decades of this has brought us to a false either/or dichotomy: rejecting the world and only concerning yourself with individual enlightenment. But what if 'enlightenment'—whatever that might be—is not *for you*? What if we are here in service to the divine world, and realization of our own divinity is not for us, but in service to the deities that give rise to us, especially the chthonic ones?

The hope is that time spent consciously aware of both the earth and the heavens as living presence will not only balance our connection to the upper and lower realms, but do something helpful for them. All traditional mythologies speak of goddesses and gods both underground and in celestial space. In spite of these mythologies being relegated to the dead story bin of our culture, the reality is that all myth is outside time, living now, always happening. Bringing the awareness of our divine connection to all these worlds into the heart of our being can only help us navigate *this* life attuned to *this* full reality within us.

Rg Veda 10.90 Puruṣa Sukta
Hymn of the Cosmic Human

Puruṣa is one thousand heads, one thousand eyes, one
thousand feet.
He is all sides of the Earth,
and stands beyond it the breadth of ten fingers.

Puruṣa, who, even now in this place, is all that has gone,
and all which is about to become; reigning over immortality,
powerful through eating food.

Puruṣa's greatness is of this measure, yet more excellent;
one quarter is all existence;
one quarter is immortal heaven.

Puruṣa moves upwards, three quarters rising,
one quarter becoming in this place.
Hence he strides in all directions,
through that which eats and that which does not eat.
From him Viraj is born, and Puruṣa from Viraj.
Thus born, he surpasses the Earth East and West.

With Puruṣa as the oblation, the gods perform the sacrifice,
with spring the clarified butter, summer the sacrificial fuel,
and autumn the offering.

Seven sticks are for enclosing the fire, three times seven sticks
are for fuel. The gods who prepare the sacrifice bind Puruṣa
as the sacrificial animal.

Puruṣa, born in the beginning,
is this sacrifice consecrated on the sacred grass.
In this way, the gods, the *sadhyas* and the *ṛṣis* sacrifice.

From this sacrifice, in which everything is cast into the fire,
the drippings are collected,
and the sacrifice is turned in to the beasts of the air, forest and village.

From this sacrifice, in which everything is cast into the fire,
hymns and chants are given birth;
and from that meter and sacrificial formulae are born.

From that horses are born, and those animals with two rows of teeth;
cows are born of that; from that are born goats and sheep.

When Puruṣa is divided, into how many parts is he separated?
What is his face? What do they call his arms, thigh and feet?

His face abides in the Brahman;
his arms are made into the warrior-princes;
his thighs are the workers;
servants are born of his feet.

The Moon is born from his mind;
the Sun is born from his eye;
Indra and Agni are from his mouth;
from his breath Vayu is born.

From his navel the intermediate atmosphere arises;
from his head the sky likewise moves;
the Earth comes from his feet; and the directions form his ear.
Thus the worlds are ordered.

With the sacrifice the gods sacrificed the sacrifice.
These are the original dharmas.
These powers reach the dome of the sky where dwell the *sadhyas*,
the ancient gods.

II. Exegeses

Orpheus mosaic from 194 BC recently returned to Turkey after being taken from Şanlıurfa.

On the right side of the well-fitted house of Hades is a spring,
and close to this spring stands a shining cypress:
Around this place the descending souls cool themselves.
Do not approach this spring.
But proceed to the lake of Mnemosyne (Memory)
with cold water flowing forth: There are guardians here:
And they will ask you with shrewd speech
what you are looking for in the darkness of deadly Hades.
Say: "I am a child of Earth and starry Heaven:
and I am parched with thirst and perishing: But give me
to drink from Mnemosyne's lake."
And they will show you to the Chthonian king:
and give you to drink from Mnemosyne's lake:
And then having drunk you will walk on the holy path of the many,
on which also other renowned mystai and bakkhoi walk

—Hipponion Orphic tablet

Exegesis of the Song 'Orpheus' by David Sylvian

David Sylvian's *Secrets of the Beehive* from 1987 is not a CD infused into the popular cultural mindscape, and not likely to generate a *33 ⅓* book, but one could guess that it makes the desert island list of everyone who has devoted time to it.

Sylvian is at his most lyrical, each note of his singing what it needs to be, a lead instrument, with the rest of the band showing it in better and better light. Now, in this musical age, twisted beats and fuzzy, glitchy production obscure lyrics. Even Sylvian himself has stopped singing, and mostly speaks avant guardedly amidst mildly-discordant electronics, with the occasional return to brilliance like 'World Citizen'.

But that was now and this is then. It is obvious that Sylvian knows that 'Orpheus' is the standout song, since these are the only lyrics reproduced in the CD booklet. (There are several serviceable live versions on youtube.) The song is in three sections, roughly analogous to a darkness-enlightenment-reintegration structure. The chorus comes in after the second and third verses, with a curious pause between the two.

Standing firm on this stoney ground
The wind blows hard
Pulls these clothes around
I harbour all the same worries as most
The temptations to leave or give up the ghost
I wrestle with an outlook on life
that shifts between darkness and shadowy light
I struggle with words for fear that they'll hear
But Orpheus sleeps on his back still dead to the world

Someone, let's say the bard, is in the midst of it. Winds of life's vicissitudes are blowing the external, with only a stoney, infertile ground to hold to. But the winds are blowing internally too: what view of life can you hold to, like a flapping cloak, when everything is dark, or at best suggestive of light?

And then the indecision of whether or not to stay the course, when your navigation depends on insight.

Is there a difference between 'leaving' and 'giving up the ghost'? Hard to say. Stop trying to do what? And what makes it a common dilemma? The last line offers a clue, the bard's 'struggle with words for fear that they'll hear'. So maybe this is about waiting for poetic inspiration, with Orpheus the muse, in a death-like sleep. Here is the sadness of the poet, pen cramped in self-reflective fear of criticism.

But there is something more in Orpheus' trance. He is not only the prototype poet-hymnodist, or singer-songwriter, but the bringer of an initiation tradition to Greece. For Orpheus, initiation transpires underground, where you unite with your true self. And if you were an ancient Greek, how would you get to the underworld? As the song says, you would lie on your back in what is called incubation, very, very still, until you basically disappear to this world and sink to Hades.

Sunlight falls, my wings open wide
There's a beauty here I cannot deny
And bottles that tumbled and crashed on the stairs
Are just so many people I knew never cared
Down below on the wreck of the ship
Are a stronghold of pleasures I couldn't regret
But the baggage is swallowed up by the tide
As Orpheus keeps to his promise and stays by my side

Boom, the moment of revelation, inspiration—you didn't even know you had wings. There is beauty in everything, including the darkness. All those people you were afraid to show your words to have fallen and crashed into insignificant shards. Everything somehow makes unitive sense and fits, even incorporating past 'lower' shipwrecked pleasures. Not only is there sunlight from above, but a rising from below, a swallowing of the past in a tide of understanding. And Orpheus is there, keeping his word as all initiates do, once there, always there.

There was a time when the bards were the mystics and the mystics were the poets and the poets were the priests and the priests were the healers and the healers were the initiators and the initiators were the bards. Poetic inspiration continuously generated a world we can barely imagine today. And we were—and are still—there amidst the mists of Vedic, Druidic and Orphic in-formed and enchanted realms, now over-towered by the gritted concrete and corroded steel of adamantine scientific separation. We've lost our red shoes and Toto is a bad defunct rock band.

The Greek chorus chimes:

Tell me, I've still a lot to learn
Understand, these fires never stop
Believe me, when this joke is tired of laughing
I will hear the promise of my Orpheus sing

The fires are eternal, the learning can never be complete, because it is alive. And the biggest joke of life, for those of us lucky enough to have it played on us, is that our ego is a real entity, and that those fearful and aggrandizing thoughts comprise who we are. Cartesian bad magic shrouds our true identity, our oneness, with the trance of individuality, and when the spell is broken, the laugh clears us for the song of Orpheus again, fresh trout from the eternal spring, the elusive red berry from the sacred font.

Sleepers sleep as we row the boat
Just you, the weather, and I gave up hope
But all of the hurdles that fell in our laps
Were just fuel for the fire and straw for our backs
Still the voices have stories to tell
Of the power struggles in heaven and hell
But we feel secure against such mighty dreams
As Orpheus sings of the promise tomorrow may bring

Your illusions of selfhood and society are laid waste. What do you do in a sleepwalker world where politics, science and religion are hopelessly irrelevant, and antithetical to in-sight? You can keep relating the true stories, the myths, the bardic poesis, even in the face of everyone feeling fully insulated against their power. The fire needs to be fed, kept aflame by the friction of our rubbing up against an insane and irredeemable corporately-generated reality. For the myths are always happening, now: Osiris is always being dis-membered by Seth and re-membered by Isis; Indra is ceaselessly slaying the dragon Vṛtra, releasing the concealed waters; and Orpheus is perpetually returning home with Eurydice.

Orpheus on his lyre, North Africa, 3rd century

Exegesis of 'Saint Stephen' by Robert Hunter and Jerry Garcia

The modern definition of an exegesis is loose enough to include an explanation and interpretation of any word, sentence or complete text, though originally refers to a treatment of scripture or sacred literature, especially biblical. Why raise what is essentially a rock and roll dance number to the level of sacred art? And further, this leads to an overwhelming question: what then is sacred art?

> Oh, do not ask, "What is it?"
> Let us go and make our visit.[49]

Noted scholar of sacred traditions, Seyyed Hosein Nasr, states flatly that "Sacred art cannot be created outside of the traditional culture for which it was meant."[50] From that vantage no one in modern 'western' society is capable of producing sacred art. Nasr continues, "However, it is possible for cosmic qualities, spiritual qualities, to be reflected through art which is not itself of a traditional nature."[51] In understanding Nasr, the word 'reflection' is important, since he feels sacred art "is the vehicle for the transmission of a knowledge which is of a sacred nature…(it) has a sacramental function, and is, like religion itself, at once truth and presence."[52]

To simplify before we go too far afield, we can provisionally say that sacred art involves some kind of direct transmission of an aspect or aspects of a traditional sacred vision, while a 'lesser' reflection of these qualities is possible outside of established orthodoxies. It would be worthwhile to consider here that implicit in these descriptions is that sacred art is sacred *for somebody*, it is not sacred in itself as an 'independent' object of consideration.

---

49 "The Love Song of J. Alfred Prufrock" by T. S. Eliot.

50 "Echoes of Infinity: An Interview with Seyyed Hosein Nasr," p. 27.

51 ibid, p. 27.

52 Nasr, *Knowledge and the Sacred*.

Is 'Saint Stephen' sacred art? This article tries to show that 'Saint Stephen' is at least reflective of the sacred, admitting that one could argue cogently that all manifestation is inherently reflective of the divine. What is important here is not definitions, but digging. Hopefully the search for wisdom in the bowels of a rock song can open the heart to other possibilities of finding the vision that underlies every moment, every thought, every dance. This exegesis begins with situating the song in the 'tradition' of the '60's.

'Saint Stephen' was recorded in 1969 during the peak of psychedelic experimentation about which much subsequently has been written and said. Frequently the adjective 'naive' precedes any discussion of that time, implying a certain 'maturity' in the subsequent fundamentalist materialistic[53] decades responsible for the revisioning. There are ever-recurring cycles of nostalgia for aspects of the '60's (even Thomas Pynchon has a film made of one of his novels!), such as tye-dyed wear, bell bottoms that don't go away, beads, and neo-psychedelic[54] bands, but interest is more a corporate search for baby boom and baby boom grandkid dollars than a sub-cultural longing for other than what society regards as a fulfilling life.

That said, the 1960's come across as more of a time of searching and questioning, when the culture of empty accumulation had reached a nadir, and more so today: when you think you have reached the bottom of the barrel, it is only the tip of the iceberg. For those searching for another way of being in this culture, it isn't the longing for something other than what the material culture has to offer that is naive. The peril for many lay in the expectation of completely finding fulfillment in something 'external': entheogens, mostly taken out of a ritual aboriginal context. Rather than becoming a vehicle for coming

---

53 A term coined by Robert Anton Wilson.

54 From the Greek words psyche, 'mind', and deloun, 'to show'. Early LSD researchers thought that it displayed the inner workings of the mind, but things are much weirder than that. Most partakers prefer 'entheogen', a substance that manifests 'god within'.

to understand and experience the Holy in one's mundane, ordinary walk through life, the hallucinogenic experience for many becomes a recreational end in itself, something to do with pretensions of revelation.

Still, for a number of individuals, the ingestion of peyote, 'sacred' mushrooms, and/or LSD radically undermined the presupposed Aristotelian and Newtonian experience of the world, consisting of independently existing 'things' and an independent 'self' moving amongst them. The hallucinogenic experience made viable other possibilities, most notable those of the Eastern traditions, which suddenly made some kind of sense.[55] A oneness underlying the normal perception of separateness emerged, a unifying vision that entheogens made one privy to, or at least hinted at.

The song 'Saint Stephen' with lyrics by Robert Hunter and performed by the Grateful Dead comes out of this time, and seems to be about someone who knows and lives through this vision.[56]

Although there are a number of saints canonized as 'Stephen' in the annals of Christianity, two are well-known. The biblical St. Stephen is mentioned briefly but importantly in the *Acts of the Apostles*. Some kind of argument broke out between the Hebrew and Greek factions of the fledgling Church concerning proper distribution to widows. Remember that the Christian sect was essentially communal at this time. Land and goods were donated to the whole, and the community took as necessary. It's a section of the *New Testament* not often visited by megachurch pastors. The apostles decided "It would be a grave mistake for us to neglect the word of God to wait at the

---

55 Aldous Huxley's *The Doors of Perception* is one of the earliest and best examples.

56 There is a loose consensus that the song celebrates Stephen Gaskin (1935-2014), who founded The Farm, one of the oldest and still successful eco-communities in 1970, and held the Monday Night Class, a large weekly eco-spiritual gathering of hippies, at the time it was written. The lyricist Robert Hunter, who rarely discusses meanings in his lyrics, leaving that up to the listener, in interviews indicates that Gaskin is not the subject of the song.

table,"[57] which meant they would appoint seven men "full of spirit and wisdom" to deal with mundane matters while they themselves prayed and ministered.

"The Stoning of Saint Stephen" by Adam Elsheimer, 1604.

"And Stephen, full of grace and power, did great wonders among the people."[58] He disputed with the Jewish hierarchy,

57 *Acts of the Apostles*, 6.2

58 *Acts*, 6.8.

was brought to trial for blasphemy, and defending himself, accused his accusers—and their fathers and forefathers—of persecuting every prophet ever sent and hypocritically not keeping to Mosaic law. At this they "ground their teeth against him." Stephen suddenly had a vision of the heavens opening, with Christ at the right hand of God. He could not, unfortunately, keep silent about it, and at his description of the vision they "stopped their ears," dragged him out of the city, and stoned him in the approving presence of Saul of Tarsus, soon to be Saint Paul. Stephen's dying voice asked the Lord to forgive his attackers.

Around the turn of the last millennium there reigned a King Stephen I of Hungary, who, in his forty-year tenure, greatly organized the country into a state of sorts, centralizing the country after Western models and opening up the sparse countryside to immigration. He aided Pope Sylvester in cementing the structure of the Catholic Church in his country, for which he received the title 'Apostolic King' and the usual posthumous sainthood.[59]

This history indirectly refers to the character Saint Stephen described in the song, in terms of sainthood in general and what exactly we are to learn from their lives. The connections are not essential to work with the song, and they are left to the reader to assemble. On to the lyrics.

Saint Stephen with a rose
In and out of the garden he goes
Country garland in the wind and the rain
Wherever he goes the people all complain

The rose of course is the transcultural workhorse of mystic symbolism, from the rosettes woven into Persian carpets to the

59 Emil Lengyel, *1000 Years of Hungary: A Short History*, p. 23-27. An interesting side note—since the Grateful Dead deeply mined American music—concerning Stephen of Hungary's son, Prince (later Saint) Emeric, whose "name was very popular in mid-fifteenth century Florence, when Amerigo Vespucci, son of Nostaggio the Notary was born. Amerigo is the Italianized form of Emeric; and thus, according to some scholars, the name of America is of Hungarian origin." p. 28.

windows of the great European Gothic cathedrals; from the poetry of Rumi and Shabistari to Dante and Blake. The single rose, as held by Stephen, indicates perfection, completion, and as with the Rosicrucians, adorns an initiate. The rose also indicates martyrdom, which is in a way an extreme form of perfection. Roses are sacred to goddesses like Aphrodite and Isis, and Lakṣmi is born of 108 large and 1008 small rose petals.

North Rose Window, Chartres Cathedral.

In the Islamic Sufi tradition, in which Allah is sometimes referred to as 'The Everlasting Rose', the Prophet Muhammed:

> ...declared the red rose to be the manifestation of God's glory. He thus gave the rose—loved by poets

throughout the world—the sanction of religious experience; his vision of God is a vision of clouds of roses, the divine presence fulgent as a marvelous red rose.[60]

Gustave Dore: Beatrice leads Dante through the Ninth Heaven, 1868.

Dante's ecstatic vision of heaven in the *Paradiso* takes the form of a white rose. In Blake's 'The Sick Rose', the 'invisible worm' of corporeal desire eats away at its perfection. The rose in western literature functions similarly to the lotus in eastern. The lotus rises unsullied from a muddy pool as pure

60 Annemarie Schimmel. *Mystical Dimensions of Islam*, p. 299.

consciousness, or a unitive vision, unaffected by yet intimately connected to the world of sense objects. Roses bloom within a tangle of thorns in much the same way.

With this in mind, 'Saint Stephen with a rose' is someone who has had—and tries to live attuned to—a vision of oneness. The 'garden' he moves 'in and out of', like Eden, or *The Rose Garden of Divine Mysteries* of Mahmud Shabistari, is a place of radical, primordial knowing: outside time, yet upon which all manifestation in time rests. Being beyond time and space, it is no-where to stay: Stephen goes in and out for renewal and remembrance. From this vision he knows what to do with his life.

Saint Stephen is a 'country garland'. In an ironic tautology, the Greek original for 'Stephen' is *Stéfanos*, which was the crown or garland of flowers given to winners of various contests and games. It may have a connection to a halo. The garland is circular, representative of perfection and eternity outside of time, yet still part of the world, the country where life is lived. The flowers of the garland are taken from the garden, wisdom to make use of in the world of 'wind and rain'—suffering, obstacles and challenges.

What chance has anyone who has *seen* to describe this vision in terms of the material world? Why does the mystic need to explain reality in terms of science? The 'people all complain' if he dares to speak of what he knows, if he gives voice to this vision of oneness. You can only complain of an other, or to an other, and no one wants to be told of their ignorance of unity, even if, and *especially* if, this knowledge leads to an end to suffering. Martín Prechtel's Tzutujil teacher put it to him thus: "Now that you're one of us, you will always feel lonely, and betrayed by what humans value, but loved by the echoing Holies. Get used to it!"[61]

Stephen prosper in his time
Well he may and he may decline

61 Martín Prechtel. *The Unlikely Peace at Cuchumaquic: The Parallel Lives of People as Plants: Keeping the Seeds Alive.*

Did it matter? Does it now?
Stephen would answer if he only knew how

In this culture, prospering is thought of in terms of monetary gain. The second line indicates either that his prosperity declines, or that he declines prosperity. There is the movement of life with its risings, fallings, comings, goings. Yet Stephen is indifferent to it. While this indifference may be antithetical to the worries and strivings of nearly all people, it is a common attribute of the unitive vision. A line from the *Bhagavad Gīta* illustrates this:

> Men of learning view with equal eye a Brahman
> of knowledge and good learning,
> A cow, and even a dog and an outcaste. (5.18)

How can the vagaries of personal accumulation matter to someone steeped in living knowledge, whose wealth is the fearless certainty of being *what is*?

The question is what to answer the 'complainers', those to whom prosperity in the material sense matters. The problem of answering occurs again later in the song. It may be that our Stephen is less than perfect and has a thing or two to learn.

Wishing well with the golden bell
Bucket hanging clear to hell
Hell halfway 'twixt now and then
Stephen fill it up and lower down
And lower down again

This verse echoes the first. Instead of going in and out of a garden, he is riding a bucket to the bottom of bottoms and back. This is a wonderful juxtaposition of images in having Stephen draw nourishment from that which is conventionally considered a place of eternal damnation. This hell, however, is not the place for some semi-incarnate sinning 'soul' to writhe in torment. Its eternality is outside of time, between 'now and then', and might be best looked at as a 'place' of primordial manifestation, the undifferentiated, from which wishes and desires are brought into being, for us and as us. What is such a place, but ourselves?

This particular well sounds a golden bell. Like the mythic Celtic wells of inspiration truth rings clearly from a drink of these replenishing waters. There is also the element of calling, giving voice to the vision, and enjoining others to participate. Next, in the song's bridge, this vision gets quite the psychedelic proclamation:

Lady finger dipped in moonlight
Writing 'What for?' across the morning sky
Sunlight splatters dawn with answers
Darkness shrugs and bids the day goodbye

Speeding arrow, sharp and narrow
What a lot of fleeting matters you have spurned
Several seasons, with their treasons
Wrap the babe in scarlet covers, call it your own

What a lovely image of lady's finger dipping into an inkwell of moonlight to write across the daybreak sky. There is even the trace of dunking a cookie in moo(n) milk. A lady-finger can also apply to either a type of grass, or anything long and slender. It also recalls the Zen adage of not mistaking the finger pointing at the moon for the moon itself, that is, preferring words or images of reality for the experience. Often, however, the moon represents indirect or reflected knowledge, the ordinary afflicted consciousness *of*, where the individual self is felt to be an entity moving about in a world composed of independently existing objects. The song questions this worldview ('what for?') by writing with evanescent moonlight as ink; in other words the mind can only frame the question in terms of how it knows what it knows: language, reflected thought.

"Luna" by Evelyn De Morgan, 1885.

The 'answer' is the splattering sunrise itself, the inspiration of dawning, the bright light of pure unreflective knowing that we might call the consciousness within, bringing light and life. The answers to the questions of the heart can never be fully rendered in language, but in vision, the sun rising again and again in an act of continuous creation which is our life. The darkness, ignorance, can only shrug, depart, and catch us next time around.

The speeding arrow is the directionality of our life. In the words of Spanish philosopher Ortega y Gasset:

> ...man has the spiritual dynamics of a released arrow that has lost sight of its target...formally pure movement, without figure or image, and movement drawn forward by a goal.[62]

Narrow with focus, Stephen gives up the transient matters of life as an end. In a way, even the seasons betray us with their constant cyclical movement, reminiscent of the opening line of T.S. Eliot's *The Wasteland,* "April is the cruellest month," where there is the personal sense of being duped by the thought of everlasting spring. We can only betray ourselves by fixing life through thought and not allowing its movement to carry us.

The 'babe in scarlet colors' could mean many things. Given that the song, titularly at the very least, is about the first Christian martyr, the swaddling Christos comes to mind, draped in the color of blood, life and passion. The color also calls to mind sacrifice, both Stephen and Christ having given lives. And that sacrifice, 'taking up the cross and following', is sacrificing the desires of our ego for higher desires. What does the Divine need of us? Personal desires are replaced by life living you, the babe reborn every moment in the temple of your body of experiential sensation. To 'call it your own' is to take responsibility for life, not as an independent manipulating 'I', but as a vision of Life itself, a movement of the totality which becomes a garden when it is known and lived as what it is. This is an awesome responsibility, since all of life is contained in every action, and, "You must act attending to no less than the holding together of the world."[63]

62 Jose Ortega y Gasset. *Historical Reason*, p. 15.

63 *Bhagavad Gītā*, 3.20.

Did he doubt or did he try?
Answers a plenty in the bye and bye
Talk about your plenty, talk about your ills
One man gathers what another man spills

There are still questions about the particulars of life. Again, do they matter? In time, all will be discussed, the ups of plenty to the downs of our ills. In all this we are interconnected. Again, a great responsibility comes with knowing this. What one does, says—or even thinks—'spills' out to affect others. Yes, the line could refer to a permaculturist utilizing what is merely waste to another, but given the rest of the song, it feels more karmic. Every action gets played out in other lives. If you are aware of this, and realize that the other is 'your own', you live through a unitive vision.

Saint Stephen will remain
All he lost he shall regain
Seashore washed by the suds and the foam
Been here so long he's got to calling it home

No effort or sacrifice on the spiritual path is wasted. Sacrifice is the operative word for a seeker of truth. At first one sacrifices time, money, 'things one would rather be doing', in order to work on oneself. One loses the conventional goals of this culture—acquisition of goods (not 'bads'), a rigid torso, fashion runway partners and other media advertis-lures. Eventually you lose even yourself as pre-existent instigator and doer of all activity.

Just about every traditional culture has a cosmogenesis story depicting emergence from the waters, and some specifically about foam, such as the birth of Aphrodite, and the earth produced from this churning foam in the *Upanisads*. This froth lies at the hazy transition between the manifest and the unmanifest, where experience comes into being. This is Stephen's home, the fractal shore between these worlds, the edge of creation as it is happening.

Fortune comes a-crawling, Calliope woman
Spinning that curious sense of your own
Can you answer? Yes I can
But what would be the answer to the answer man?

Fortune—the real fortune of embodied wisdom—is acquired slowly through repeated spiritual practice ('been here so long…'). Calliope is the muse of epic poetry and eloquence, also the mother of the original singer and songwriter, Orpheus. She is also the specific muse called by the mystic magical philosopher Empedocles to enable him to perfectly convey what needs saying in his poetry.[64] Maybe more germane to the paisley '60's, a calliope is also a wild steam-driven organ bringing a circus sound to the streets, and used here as a carnival depiction of the Goddess in flower, comprised of oneself as the world. The 'curious' sense is that it is your world, that she is dancing just for you. It is generated through your own particular past which filters and colors—be they pastels or day-glo—life in the moment, as it arises for and as each of us. The 'I' singing the song can now answer because she or he has, through the recollection of the vision as the song, joined with Stephen. The answer comes not in words, but through a life lived in consonance with this vision. Never can we get 'behind' our lives: our life is already here. There is no answer to the answer.

To answer the original question vis a vis 'Saint Stephen' and sacred art, it seems evident this song is a depiction of a sacred vision, loosely connected to the edge-of-death vision of the stoned Christian martyr, reflecting qualities of the sacred through the prism of poetic language. The metaphors are both traditional—a rose, a well—and innovative—a ladyfinger, a calliope. While nodding to the past, its expression is sifted

64 Robert Hunter, who wrote these lyrics, has long been devoted to the muses. He begins the epic song cycle "Terrapin Station" with this evocation:
Let my inspiration flow
In token lines suggesting rhythm
That will not forsake me
Till my tale is told and done…

through the cultural period of its birth. Although it is moot whether or not, in order to satisfy Nasr's criteria, sacred knowledge has been transmitted to qualify it as sacred art, certainly there is a 'truth and presence' to the song, especially in a concert setting. The music has elements of a march and jig, which makes it danceable in an odd way. Continuously searching for the vision is what being on a spiritual path denotes, and as we go probing for it, may it come looking for us.

"Calliope Teaching Orpheus" by Alexandre Auguste Hirsch, 1865.

108 Mysterium

One of the great cosmic numbers is 108, showing up in just about every aspect of sacred geometry study. It's important to remember that the qualities of 108 resonate with all its multiples of ten, such as 1080, 10,800, and 108,000. These collected correspondences are offered for your consideration and meditation.

Number & Music
$1^1 \times 2^2 \times 3^3 = 108$

108 is the product of the first three numbers times themselves.

$108 = 2 \times 54 = 3 \times 36 = 4 \times 27 = 6 \times 18 = 9 \times 12$

$1080 = 72 \times 15 = 3 \times 360°$ circuit

The factors of 108 can be divided nicely into all the major harmonic proportions – (2/3, 3/4) to give you the perfect fourth and fifth of the octave.

108 = sum of the first nine multiples of three:
$0 + 3 + 6 + 9 + 12 + 15 + 18 + 21 + 24 = 108$

In the category of 'close enough', if you take the fraction 1/109, you get a repeating decimal of 108 digits, the last six of which are the first six of the Fibonacci sequence in reverse.

Some musicians prefer to tune to the cosmic A432 cycles/second (4×108) rather than the standard equal temperament A440.

Geometry
The inscribed angle of a pentagon is 108° :

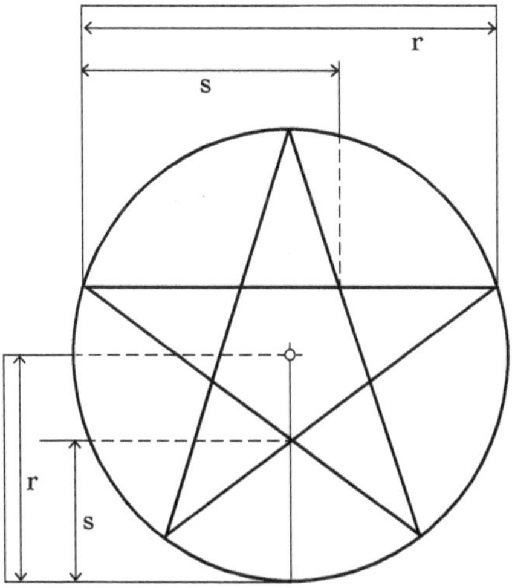

$$\frac{r}{s} = \phi$$

$$\phi = 1.618$$

The Pentagon and The Golden Triangle

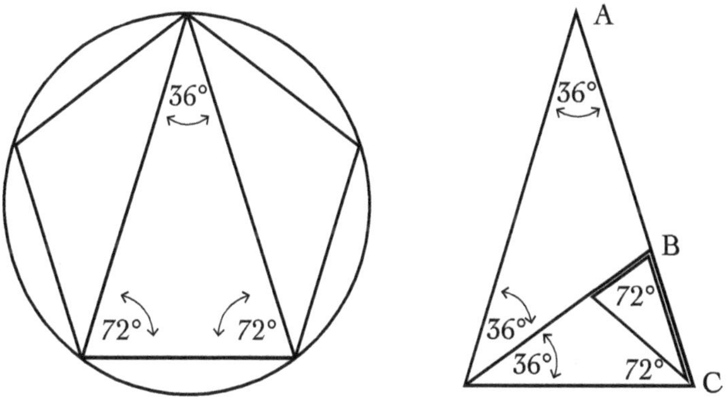

108° is the complement to the 72° - 72° - 36° Golden triangle, inscribed within the pentagon. Each cut of the pentagram yields the Golden Mean proportion.

Angles of the pyramid total 1080° (four triangular faces: 4 × 180° = 720° plus the square base of 360°).

Total number of degrees in a cube is 2160° (2 × 1080°).

A circle has 360° × 60 minutes = 216,000 minutes. A dome (semi-circle) then has 108,000 minutes.

The equation 2 sin (108°/2) = ϕ (the golden ratio)

Cosmology

The radius of the moon = 1080 miles.

The diameter of the sun is 108 times greater than the diameter of the earth.

108 times the diameter of the sun = distance of the sun to the earth.

108 times the diameter of the moon = distance of the moon to the earth.

This remarkable 'coincidence' of 108 discs of the sun fitting between here and there, and also 108 discs of the moon fitting between here and there, is responsible for the even more interesting coincidence of both sun and moon appearing to be the same size from earth. We don't think about it, but it is remarkable that the sun and moon cover each other exactly during eclipses, *from our perspective*.

108 million roman half-paces = circumference of the earth.

2 × 10,800 mph = speed of the sun around the galactic core.

The orbit of Saturn is 10,800 days.

The diameter of the earth (7920 mi.) + the diameter of the moon (2160) = 10,080.

There are 108 sacred stars in Taoist astrology.

In Vedic astrology, besides the 12 sign zodiac, there is a 27 sign lunar (*nakṣatra*) zodiac, with each sign being divided into 4 *pada*s (steps), giving you 108 steps to enlightenment along this celestial path.

$108 \times \pi = 339$, a number used in the construction of the Vedic fire altar, also signifying the number of discs the sun traces across the sky from sunrise to setting.

Time

Heraclitus reputedly said that civilization is destroyed every 10,800 years.

1080 *minums* in a Hebrew hour.

1080 human breaths per hour (18/minute).

$1080 \times 24 = 25{,}920$ breaths in a day.

$108 \times 240 = 25{,}920$ years, or the time of the precession of the equinoxes or Great Platonic year. The number of breaths in a day equals the number of years in a complete cycle. The human and cosmic are connected intimately.

$108 \times 20 = 2160$ or a great month, the time spent in the age of a particular zodiacal sign (we are moving out of Pisces into Aquarius now).

There are 108 days from All Souls Day to Christmas, a movement from darkness to light.

108 intersects the Yugas in interesting ways:

Yuga	Divine Years	Human Years	DY/108	HY/108
Kali	1200	432,000	1.111	400
Dvapara	2400	864,000	2.222	800
Tretā	3600	1,296,000	3.333	1200
Kṛta	4800	1,728,000	4.444	1600

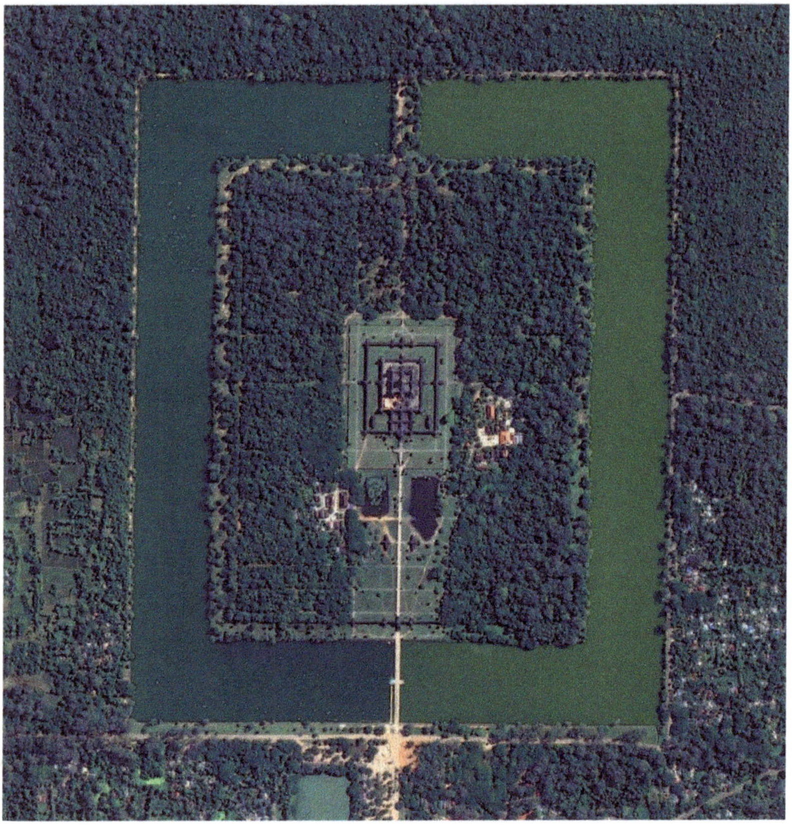

The various enclosures of Angkor Wat represent each of the Yugas.
The height of the temple is 108 cubits high.

One divine year equals 360 human years. The divine years in a yuga divided by 108 set up a lovely 'infinite tetractys' of repeating decimals. There are 1,296,000 seconds in a 360° circle (360° × 60 min × 60 secs). There are 864,000 seconds in the 24-hour day (864,000 miles is the diameter of the sun). There are also 108 yugas in a mahayuga, or complete time cycle, from the beginning of time to the complete reabsorption of everything back into the one, the whole cycle being merely an eyeblink of Brahmā. One can explore these numbers indefinitely, but what is clear is the connection of cosmic time to cosmic space through the number 108.

Vedic/Buddhist

108 shows up most overtly in the Vedic and Buddhist cultures. There are 108 mala beads in their rosary, 108 names for Viṣṇu and Śiva, 108 traditional *Upaniṣads,* 10,800 bricks used in the construction of the Vedic fire altar, and 10,800 verses in the *Ṛgveda* ('praise of wisdom'). Multiplied by the 40 syllables in each stanza, you get 432,000, or the number of years in the Kali Yuga. 108 is inherent in much temple and stupa architecture, see especially the complexes at Angor Wat and Angor Thom, where the towers were built 108 cubits tall based on the measure of each particular king's elbow to fingertip.[65] There are 108 Arhats of the Buddha, 108 forms in traditional Indian dance, 108 *marmas*—energy centers in the subtle body, 108 gopis following Kṛṣṇa, and on New Years in Japan, temple gongs are sounded 108 times.

Greek Gematria

Gematria is the tradition of assigning number totals to specific letters, mostly found in the ancient Greek, Babylonian, Hebrew and Arabic. Totals for words and phrases that are very close together indicate a strong spiritual relationship between them. There is a certain 'horseshoes' rule in gematria wherein being within one or two of the number in question yields the same harmonic resonance.[66]

1080 = the Holy Spirit (*haghia pneuma*)
= the Earth Spirit (*gaia pneuma*)
= the virgin deity of earth
= fountain of wisdom (*sophia*)
= netherworld (*tartaros*)
= bridegroom (name given to one on return from initiation)
= Mary (192) + Jesus (888)

65 Eleanor Mannikka, *Angkor Wat: Time, Space, and Kingship.*

66 The following are taken from John Michell's *The Dimensions of Paradise.* He sees 108 as a lunar number—for example, the atomic mass for silver is 108.

1081 = the abyss
= the satyrs
1082 = prophesy
= *iatromantis* healer-priest
1079 = Chiron
= the divine measure

Most of these correspondences are connected with deep feminine earth wisdom, and probably our greatest loss in western culture—initiation. Ancient initiations took place in the underworld, and were presided over by a feminine deity. These words harmonizing around 1080 indicate the place of initiation, the deity involved, the name given the initiated, the priest of the initiation and the wisdom obtained.

Conclusion

There are certain correspondences that are hard to signify, such as the 108 suitors of Penelope in the *Odyssey,* or the 108 stitches on a baseball, and they go on and on. What makes 108 so special is how it is woven into all aspects of human sacred experience, from the dimensions of the cosmos, to the division of time, to the human body and its ultimate connection to the spirit or *pneuma*, the breath. It is no wonder then that doing an activity 108 times sacralizes it, that is, carries it from the human realm into the cosmic, bringing human experience into resonance with and remembrance of that which is always already divine within and without.

Pythagoras Played Centerfield: The Veiled Sacred Geometry of Baseball

Every devoted fan understands something inexplicably special—and implicitly mystical for some—about the game of baseball lacking in other sports. It certainly has inspired more literature than other sports. And there is a deep structural and symbolic integrity underlying the mythic, poetic, ritual and dramatic dimensions of the game that connect its fans in a way akin and related to ancient Greek theater. The word fan, shortened from 'fanatic', comes from Latin '*fanaticus*', which means 'pertaining to a temple', or '*fanum*'. Even the word 'enthusiasm' means to be possessed by a divinity.

Although desacralization runs the game today, and there is no clear origin story for the game in its current form, a certain sacred architecture structuring baseball may be elucidated through the discipline of sacred geometry. The peculiar configurations of a baseball field resonate with transcendent truths about the organization of the cosmos—Greek for 'beautiful arrangement'—and the movement from the one into the many of this lived place through qualitative Pythagorean numerics. Baseball mirrors and explicates the play of the transcendent and the temporal in its field dimensions, the geometric proportion of its out—and in—lines, these numbers informing the rules and the very human activity of the game itself.

Cosmogony

In sacred geometry the one, the origin, or monad, can be rendered as a point, circle or sphere. Everything comes from and is integral to the one. It is absolute and beyond quality. It all begins, not at home, but with the pitcher (even #1 on the scorecard), the singular point from which the whole of baseball emanates. In order for the game, or manifestation, to ensue, there has to be a self-sacrifice. The one must give up absoluteness and stillness to become the many. The pitcher must let go and put the ball in play.

This pitcher stands upon a mound, the *axis mundi* at the heart of creation, holding a point, a sphere. According to Mircea Eliade, the *axis mundi,* or sacred mountain, is the meeting place of heaven, earth and hell.[67] Out of the vortical spin of the wind-up, the released ball quickly creates the space it traverses, like Zeus tossing thunderbolts from Olympus. One dimension is now two as the arrow of the ball becomes a line. The point moves toward duality (#2, the catcher). This thread from pitcher to catcher is the octave upon which all possibilities of baseball emerge, each game its own song: comedic, dramatic or tragic.

The hitter is the third dimension, holding a bat, which is the line again represented. All geometric space is birthed through the point and line. Once the ball is hit into fair (sacred) territory, three-dimensional space is generated, and the whole field comes into movement and being, until the point/ball is returned to the origin/pitcher, again and again. Each emergence from endless possibility is a completely new celestial configuration, followed by a return to the source. No two ground balls, fly balls, outs or base hits are the same.

Like any traditional sacred building, the baseball field is oriented along the cardinal directions, home being west and second base east. This alignment makes perfect cosmological sense, as the batter faces east, the direction of the rising sun and creation, from whence each pitch emerges and play dawns. Most stadia are open to the east, as if to enchant Aurora, goddess of the dawn and lover of mortal heroics, into its temple precincts.

---

67 Mircea Eliade, *The Myth of the Eternal Return: Or, Cosmos and History*, p. 12-13. A temple, church or mosque is considered to be this convergence of the worlds. One thinks of the inexplicable Dantian sufferings of Chicago Cubs fans compared to the Dionysian revelries of each year's World Series winners. Also, baseball lore is rife with religious terms. The word fan comes from the Latin *fanum*, a temple; the greatest players are 'enshrined' in The Baseball Hall of Fame in Cooperstown, NY, tantamount to Olympus.

Metrology

The Tao begets one. One begets two. Two begets three.
Three begets the ten thousand things.
– Lao-Tse, *Tao Te Ching* 42

The baseball field and rulebook guidelines are entirely constructed with three's and four's. Three is the first actualization of the potential held within the one. The one divides in two, divine masculine and divine feminine, consciousness and manifestation in potential. It takes a third to manifest a proportion, a limiting vibration from which all actualization of unlimited potential comes into being. And the rest, the ten thousand things, ensue. While three is the number of balance, harmony of opposites, the logos and pattern of being, three squared and cubed are its higher resonances. Three are the number of strikes per out; three are the number of outs per inning. Three squared gives you the nine innings per regulation game, and three cubed gives the twenty-seven outs per game.

Nine, which Annemarie Schimmel[68] calls 'the magnified sacred 3', is the number of completion, the last of the single digits. Tradition bursts with triple threes: nine orders of the Dionysian angelic hierarchy; nine Greek muses; the three-fold triple Celtic goddess; the nine terra-centric spheres of the classical and medieval universe: the seven visible planets plus the level of fixed stars plus the empyrean; the three books of thirty-three cantos of Dante's *Divina Commedia*; the nine-by-nine Hindu temple plan of Vastu; and back home with the nine openings in the human body. The bases are set at 90° right angles, 90 feet apart, a perfect square. The pitcher's mound has a nine-foot radius, and the baseball a nine-inch circumference. Within the 27 outs per team, a 'perfect' perfect game might consist of nine pitches, or three strikeouts, per inning, lasting 81 or 3^4 pitches.

68 *The Mystery of Numbers*, Chapter 9. This is a great introduction and compendium of the use and interpretation of sacred numbers across many cultures.

It is always worth remembering that for the Pythagoreans, number is not mere additive quantity but resonates spiritual quality itself, not just a representation of it. In traditional temple, church and cathedral building, using specific numbers and ratios not only represents the intended qualities. Their very presence *is* that spiritual quality, perceivable to anyone open to it. In all ancient traditions, a proscribed deity is said to inhabit a sculpture, painting or temple created through the correct proportions.

With the four bases come the earth, the elements, differentiated from the celestial number three. In fact, there is always an area of earth around the bases. Four is stability and materialization. But running the bases, one does not *square* them, but *circle* them. The combination of circle and square is the coalescence of heaven and earth, the sacred marriage or *hieros gamos*. Of course the ultimate goal is to return to the origin, to come home, not as you were when you began, but with an addition, or run. Or maybe you have performed the benevolent act of getting a hit with someone already on base, and sending them home.

Interestingly, one who circles the bases after hitting a home run travels 399 feet in rounding the bases. This is the approximate average distance a home run ball travels into the stands, again correlation of the circle and the line. Thus the batter runs the same distance he has hit the ball. Linear distance base to base is of course 360 feet, which is the short distance of a home run down most foul lines.

Four balls and three strikes are allotted to a batter. Strikes are related to time and balls to space. Three strikes resonate with the number of outs allowed a team, as each out is another tick of baseball's mythic time clock. The only other major sports to operate without a limiting stopwatch are tennis and baseball's balmy cousin, cricket. Time only moves in terms of outs. Hits, walks, runs and errors are the movement of transience within the context of timelessness. As Plato said, "Time is the moving image of eternity." A game theoretically can last forever, but never does. Baseball beautifully straddles both worlds, imaginative and linear.

The four balls also relate to the four bases and the creation of baseball's ceremonial space. Interestingly, there is a different level of intensity and anticipation when the batter is on the verge, having two strikes rather than three balls. This may be related to the generation of hope in the face of adversity, in the fans. The greatest players get hits in one-third of their plate appearances, the average players one out of four. That range expresses threes and fours again. With failure more likely, the fan is always hoping against the odds. An expectation of success would not create the same tension.

Although there are some who hold that baseball is an exercise in esoterica devised by the Masons,[69] where the bases are the traditional square and open compass in quadrilaterality, and with the gentle outfield fence the heavenly realms, there is no obvious evidence supporting this. Excepting, possibly, the elaborate dugout ritual handshakes. One can only imagine the secret ones. Still, one cannot draw the traditional baseball field without a compass and straight-edge.

The Sphere

> *The earth, when looked at from above, is like one of those balls which have leather coverings in twelve pieces.*
>
> – Plato, *Phaedo*

The baseball itself is comprised of wound yarn encircled by two interlocking torus-shaped cuts of leather (see fig. 1). The torus, drawn by moving a circle about a circle, or more prosaically, a doughnut, is connected macroscopically with phenomena such as black holes and the generation of space-time in theoretical physics, and microscopically found in electron spin and cellular reproduction. That they overlap perpendicularly again

69 See, for example, <http:prisonplanet.com/analysis_lavello_051403_occult.html> for this perspective.

shows the forces of the *axis mundi*, the immanent—manifest, mundane—pierced by the transcendent—timeless, spiritual.

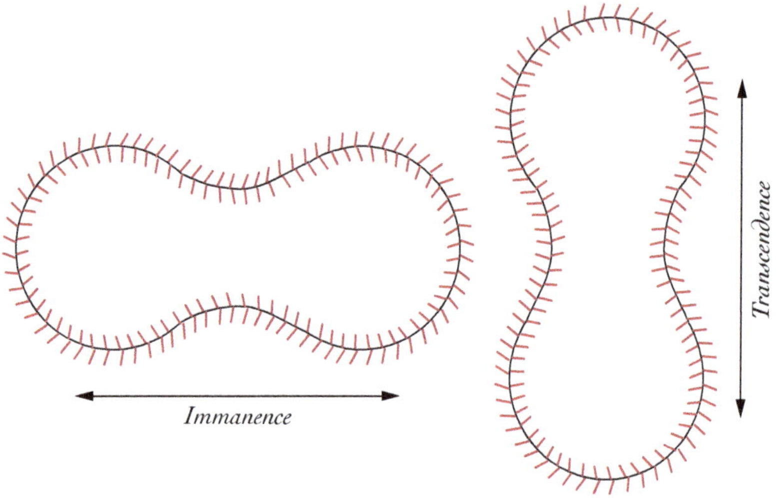

fig. 1 The unstitched baseball.

These torii are stitched 108 times to enclose the baseball, which is especially significant, as 108 is one of the mystic numbers *par excellence*.[70] For example, in India, 108 is integral to all temple and Vedic altar construction, not to mention the vast time scales of the yugas. There are 10,800 stanzas in the Rig Veda, and everyone carries around mala beads totaling 108. There are 108 auspicious signs on each of the Buddha's feet. Essentially, doing something 108 times brings it to the attention of the gods.

Curiously, astronomically, if you multiply the diameter of the sun by 108, you get its distance from the earth. If you multiply the diameter of the moon by 108, again you get *its* distance to the earth. 108 is one of those numbers that gets sacred geometers giddy.

---

70 See the previous chapter, '108 Mysterium'.

Thought Experiment

So fair and foul a day I have not seen.
– *Macbeth* I.3

Space, the field of play itself, is divided into sacred and profane, fair and foul. From the apex of home plate, fair (sacred) space is generated by two foul lines—which are actually in fair territory—at ninety-degree angles, moving northeast and southeast. One would then surmise that one-quarter of space is fair, and three-quarters foul (profane). And while the field of ritual play is circumscribed by a circular outfield enclosure, a ball hit beyond that wall occupies an intermediate zone. A ball hit there, a home run, is both in fair play, and a space occupied by fans. Those seats are traditionally the least expensive and most enthusiastic places in the stadium.

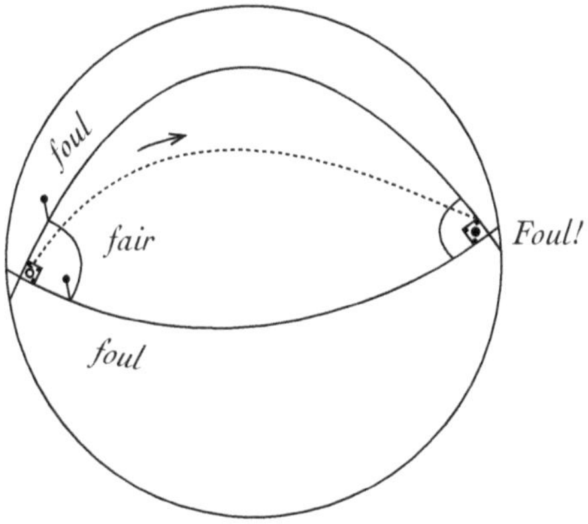

fig. 2 You can hit a ball too far.

However, there is an assumption that the base lines travel past the foul (fair) poles as far as can be imagined. There is no such thing as hitting a home run *too far*. Or is there? What is intriguing is that if you continue to extend the foul lines, they will eventually circumscribe the earth, resulting in their meeting again *behind* home plate (see fig. 2). They will cross, however, at the exact opposite point on the globe, whereupon the imaginary full connection of a Walter Johnson fastball with a Mickey Mantle swing, hit to dead center and traveling more than half way around the earth, would be foul. Also, for the sake of geometric balance, it is comforting that every baseball field initiates an anti-field on the other side of the world.

Systemic Anomaly: American League

The designated hitter rule is not only 'ritually incorrect'[71] but an atonal abomination. Anyone who comes to bat is attempting to traverse a four-stage initiation, returning home, as T.S. Eliot famously puts it, "to know the place for the first time." He or she must overcome the three inner(field) and outer(field) guardians of the thresholds, along with the two members of the battery (pitcher and catcher), and then in turn guard that same space on defense. The DH, adding an extra player, goes against the harmonic of nine. It places two players in a non-consequential limbo for half the game each: one batter does not play defense, and the pitcher does not bat and face his opposite pitcher. Here two halves do not equal one, and the mirror between offense and defense is distorted. The greatness of baseball is that it overcomes this systemic anomaly, but American League baseball is just that much less sacred, not to mention less strategically interesting, due to it.

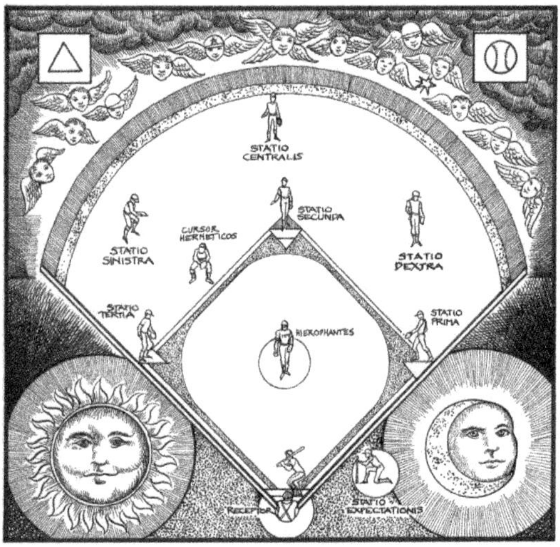

Baseball's Hermetic Field by Hannah Shapiro.

71 Hannah M.G. Shapero, "The Diamond Way: Baseball as an Esoteric Ritual." "Pythagoras Played Centerfield" is inspired by and a companion to her wonderful elucidation of baseball's Hermetic ritual underpinnings. Thanks for permission from her to use her illustration of the Hermetic Baseball Diamond. The article can be found here: southerncrossreview.org/53/diamond2.html.

Proportion

> *Proportion…is the key to arriving at a transcendental unity from the polarity of existence. Thus proportion as it has been consciously employed in an architectural or structural sense is traditionally symbolic of the Gnostic function. Indeed, ultimately, the transcendental, proportional ratios* (√2, √3, √5, and [phi/golden mean])*…are metaphysical principles which may be embodied in matter to give it significance and enable the part to contribute to and relate to the whole.*
>
> – Keith Critchlow[72]

The absolute indicator of traditional sacred space is its use of transcendental—profanely called 'irrational'—proportions. These are ratios that do not divide evenly and whose decimal remainders do not repeat as they drift off into infinity. Pi's 3.141…is the most famous. The others that frequent all traditional art and architecture are √2 (1.1412…), √3 (1.7320…), √5 (2.2360…), and especially phi, or the golden mean (1.6180…).[73]These are integral to any comprehension of Platonic, Pythagorean, Babylonian, Egyptian or Islamic expression of how divine light emanates and crystallizes as our perceived manifest order. Even though a mere piecemeal understanding of this requires a lengthy dedicated study, something can be expressed.

---

72 Keith Critchlow, "The Platonic Tradition on the Nature of Proportion," p. 135, in Christopher Bamford, ed., *Homage to Pythagoras*.

73 One of the most elegant, magical and mysterious mathematical procedures involves what happens when one adds these transcendental ratios. Add the square roots of 1, 2, 3, 4, and 5 to the golden mean ratio (ϕ):

$\sqrt{1} = 1.00000$
$\sqrt{2} = 1.41421$
$\sqrt{3} = 1.73205$
$\sqrt{4} = 2.00000$
$\sqrt{5} = 2.23607$
$\underline{\phi = 1.61803}$
10.00036

√2 is the diagonal of a square, carries the quality of generation, and is especially seen in mosques and Islamic tile design, and Eastern temples and mandalas. Medieval cathedral ground plans and sculpture use the harmonious quality of √3 to express Christ's role as intercessor between God and man, especially when depicted within fish-shaped *vesica pisces*, most notably at Chartres Cathedral.

Christ within the *vesica pisces* surrounded by the cardinal constellations matching the four canonical gospels, Chartres Cathedral, West Portal.

King Solomon's temple and the King's chamber of the Great Pyramid at Giza express √5 via the double square. The golden mean, related to √5 (phi =1+√5/2), is expressed in nearly every relation within the human body and plant kingdom, and is fabulously visualized in the facades of the Parthenon and Notre Dame of Paris.

Where can we find these relationships on the diamond? If we use the ninety-foot distance between the bases as our 'base-ic' unit, that is, 1, certain relationships among the fielders emerge (see fig. 3). The throw from third to first across the diamond, and the throw from the catcher to second trying to cut down a base stealer, are both then √2. The longest infield throw, which the shortstop makes from deep in the hole on the outfield grass, works out to be √3. A normal throw from the second baseman to first is 1/√2. The typical throw from left or right field to second base is very close to phi, while the center fielder's toss is √2. One of baseball's more exciting plays, the right fielder's throw to catch a runner advancing from first to third on a base hit, measures √5. Also, with a hit to the outfield gap that results in a play at the plate, the cutoff man, usually second baseman or shortstop, is in a golden mean relationship between the outfielder and the catcher. Finally, a foul pole 348 feet from home plate is in a relationship of pi.

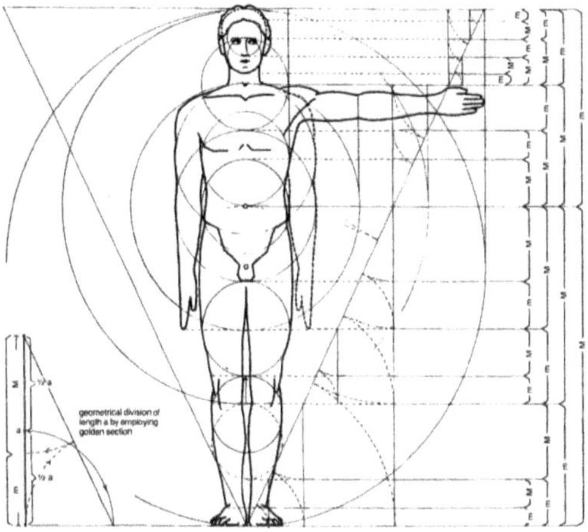

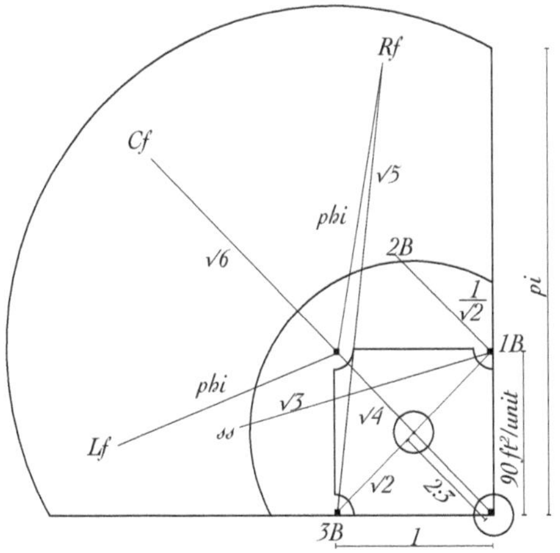

fig. 3 Baseball's proportional realtionships.

It would be nice to find an important harmonic between the 60 feet 6 inches from the pitching rubber to home plate and the 90 feet of the base paths. Apparently an original distance in the nineteenth century was 55 feet, which would bring the ratio very close to the golden mean. The current distance gives a ratio close to 2:3, which is a perfect musical fifth.

Last Licks

You can look it up.

– Casey Stengel

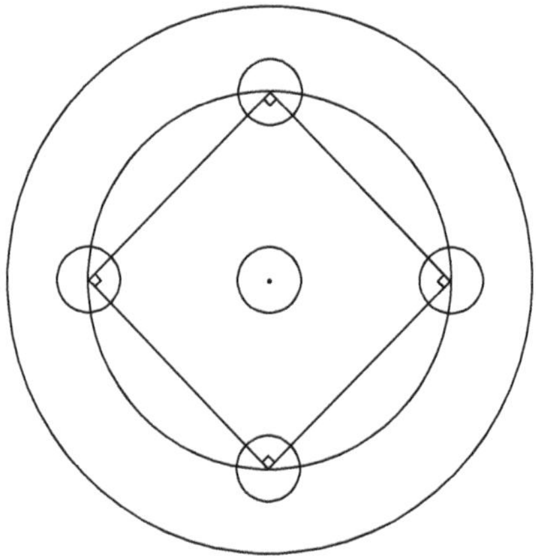

fig. 4 Baseball's mandala.

Obviously none of the preceding is a prerequisite to the pleasure of playing or watching baseball. One can walk all day through Chartres Cathedral in a sort of rapture, with no idea that a significant part of the beauty that one resonates with comes from the conscious orchestration of harmonic proportions by unnamed mystic master artists and architects. It seems that part of the deep, mythic and even archetypal love that baseball engenders comes from its beautiful mandalic countenance (see fig. 4), harmonic structuring and numeric symmetry. And baseball time is its own time, and our time being 'at the park' is ours alone, apart from the pressured hammering of clocks, flowing instead with the drift of mythic history, of heroes, villains and fate, of evanescent successes and failures, bringing us always to a new spring dawn, a new season, alike and utterly different from all before it.

III. Retroduction

Parmenides statue in the Velia Archeological Park, Italy.

It never was
and never will be because it is now, all together,
one, holding to itself. For what possible birth of it
will you look for? In what way could it have grown?
From what?

– Parmenides of Velia

Immortals become mortals, mortals become immortals:
they live in each other's death and die in each other's life.

– Heraclitus of Ephesus

Purgito Ergo Sum

We sit in a circle, waiting, in darkness near absolute. Our chairs are made as comfy as possible with an armada of pillows, cushions, blankets, throws and artfully scrunched down sleeping bags. Within the dangle of an arm are a water bottle and a sea-green plastic bucket, something you might use to mold the turrets of sandcastles fabricated as a child.

We are in a roomy apartment over a garage on a beautiful Florida estate, fantastically isolated on a lake, hermetically removed from the main drag franchise glare that scares and unsettles me far more than this unknown inner journey I await. We have just gone up one by one, ten of us, and quietly downed about a double shot glass full of ayahuasca, poured by Don Guillermo, a Shipibo *curandero* (guide, healer) or *ayahuasquero* (shaman) from Peru. For six of us it is the first time, and for three the first with any entheogen ('manifesting the divine within') or psychedelic. It is not as bitter as expected and the murky brown brew goes down smoothly. Don Guillermo must be a good chef.

Don Guillermo begins a lilting breathy whistle, blown over a bottle, sculpting the dark bardo into a sonant mandala, and the actual texture of reality subtly shifts. A presence is called in, potent and barely perceptible…and we unmoor…

An hour before we irrevocably set sail, we had gathered in the room after some time during the day getting to know each other a bit. Most of us had been observing rather limited food intake for two weeks, avoiding within reason salt, fats, spices, sugar, meat except freshwater fish, and carbs, partly as purification of the body-temple, and partly to avoid food inhibiting the plant's action. For Alethea, my wife, and I, this meant bizarrely continuous hunger in the face of nearly continuous ingestion, and we look forward to slathering something with butter afterwards almost as much as the ayahuasca journey. It took a while before I noticed Don Guillermo sitting in the corner. Apparently invisibility is one of his strengths—a useful talent when crossing borders. He is dressed innocuously in gray sweatpants and light green T-shirt. Kal, an American who has been working with Don Guillermo for twenty years, serves as translator and second *ayahuasquero*. He eerily resembles Timothy Leary.

We learn a few things. The *curandero* serves as healer, teacher, marriage counselor, therapist, exorcist, etc. within the Shipibo community. Ayahuasca (Quechua for 'vine of the spirits') is the name both for the entire potion, and one of the ingredients, the helical vortex-shaped *Banisteriopsis caapi* vine. This inactivates the stomach enzyme monoanimine oxidase (MAO), allowing the potent psychoactive dimethyltriptamine (DMT) found in many plants—in this case a small bush called *Psychotria viridis*—to circulate into the brain. This particular batch has added small amounts of *brugmansia* (datura) and what we hear as 'bohinsana', a watery plant that is not further identified.

Another of the names for ayahuasca is *la purga*, which accounts for the beach buckets. Vomiting is normal, a good thing, and any visions within temporal proximity of the purge are often significant. There's no telling who will or won't spew. Ten people will have ten very divergent experiences. Some may need extra doses to get 'drunk' and some may not get high at all. For some it may be intensely visual, and for others emotional. It will usually take about a half-hour to take effect, become almost unbearably intense for another half-hour, followed by a plateau of several hours when most of the insights are gained.

We were asked weeks ago to focus on an intention for the ceremony. This gives a focus to rebound to in case one gets lost in the sandstorm of impressions. It delineates the difference between recreational and sacramental use of entheogens. We go around the room voicing our experience and intentions. Sheryl, who has done other psychedelics, is looking for a healing. Jan is going to be spending two weeks in the jungle working with ayahuasca and other plants with Don Guillermo and would like to be prepared for the journey. She has done ayahuasca once before. Alethea, who has never tried anything stronger than marijuana, sits directly across from me and asks to experience the Divine within and to learn about healing. Marla (first time) and her brother Jack (partner of Jan and also going to the jungle in three months) are looking to clear blockages. Kristen, a young woman with a three-month-old baby (her husband is with the baby in the main house) looks for a healing. It is her first experience. Sally, who has done this maybe ten times, wants to connect strongly with the plant itself. Talpo, her husband and the organizer, is working with Pythagorean bio-mathematical epiphanies gleaned from a session two days prior. I announce that I am an ayahuasca 'virgin', which when translated by Kal gets a good laugh from Don Guillermo. His laugh, which we are soon to hear a lot of, is clear, joyous and infectious, pure as a child's. As much as I thought of my intention, it always came back to two seemingly general questions: Who am I? and What am I to do with this life? My friend Catherine sitting to my left, the eldest participant, is looking to work through old karma. Since this is her first experience of this sort, I feel she is in for a rough night. The couple whose home this is are 'sitting', that is, they sit just outside the circle, holding flashlights and ready to assist with any contingencies such as the need to find the bathroom (*la purga* is often bidirectional) or whatever might require a sober steady hand.

There are not many questions. Sheryl asks about the legality of ayahuasca. DMT is a schedule I drug and hence classified with heroin, LSD and cocaine. No point getting into the idiotic war on *some* drugs here, suffice it that our hubris in making any plant illegal astonishes me, as if the divine somehow erred in placing them within reach on this planet. We are all appreciative of Don Guillermo's risk in bringing the ayahuasca. I intuit that a good shaman's plant allies would alert him about dangerous times to travel, but maybe this is just wishful thought.

We are asked to remain seated other than bathroom visits. Not a great idea to have a bunch of loopy tripsters crossing paths while exhibiting impaired motor control. The opportunity will be given for a second or third dose if needed, as long as one waits until a song is finished or some kind of break. The *icaros*, or songs, offered by the *ayahuasquero* are a mix of Spanish, Quechua and other noises designed to entice the spirits. Don Guillermo also has a variety of panpipes and something that resembles a large ukulele and sounds like a bright mandolin. Kal has some Tibetan bowls and a bullroarer. At the end of the ceremony a candle will be lit, after which we can re- or disassemble further, or walk, or talk, or sleep. Breakfast is slated for 8:30 after which we will gather and process as much or little as we would like.

Don Guillermo opens by blowing a mist from what is apparently a bottle of cheap aftershave to the four directions. We pass around a sage smudge lit by Kal and then the bottle to anoint our head, hands and necks. We go up one by one counterclockwise to take the ayahuasca from a small glass with a handle on it. We return to our sea of pillows and get our bodies as comfortable and out of the way as possible.

Something alters dramatically with Don Guillermo's whistling song. Silence has become a roar as the curtain of time opens to let in an influx of perceptions so bodily intense, so fast that it is like trying to open your eyes under a raging waterfall and see individual droplets, or a blast of wasabi that doesn't abate. In the midst of running the rapids there is a completely lucid part of me conscious. "Holy shit, is it going to be like this for four hours?" Don Guillermo is now singing a song, incredibly beautiful, 'ayahuasca' being the only word recognized. I am up the creek and this is my paddle.

Soon what is going on visually takes precedence. Eyes open, closed, glasses on or off I *see* the same. The fabric of being is overtly geometric, fluid, and apparently fond of fluorescent colors. Swirls, circles, ovals and dots of blues, pinks, yellows and greens glowing as under a blacklight, shifting and shimmering. It is a living pattern and I can only experience astonishment in its presence. A bronze moire beehive pattern seems to hold everything together. I have somehow acquired a zoom function and move back to view the hexagons rolling and waving and then move into an individual compartment inspecting its waxy smoothness. I note that I am mildly nauseous.

Don Guillermo is playing a melody on his mandolin, and I am pulled out of my visual rapture by the sound of Catherine retching to my left. He twangs some dissonant notes and I am not sure if they are to help her through, help us to ignore it, or both. She is so consumed by vomiting that she needs help connecting with her bucket. I am totally helpless. I know she has help and that this is something she needs to go through. She doesn't need a well-meaning drunken fool blathering in blips and tripping over floating mitochondria. So I open my heart and send love not knowing the possibilities of reception, but knowing she is all right.

I am aware of my connectedness with everyone and everything. To the right of me a voice is answering Don Guillermo's songs, echoing some of his words, giggling and repeating a hiss that sounds like *hsssssaaah!* Their interplay goes on intermittently during a good part of the evening. It is obvious to me in my condition that some spirit is present but I've no idea who or why or what. That's why we do this with a shaman. He has experience with these sort of things. Kal asks if anyone needs a second dose. I am flying and the idea seems ludicrous. Four or so people go up. I wonder where they are with this. Did they get off?

Kal's voice, slow and sweet, announces that this might be a good time for a story. He wears a long striped robe that flows in weird graceful staccato as he walks. His first few words are garbled, as if I have to retune some receiving apparatus first in order to comprehend English. His tale, adumbrated here, is about establishing criteria for radically paring down your stuff to one suitcase in the face of an immanent move. You have the plane tickets, you are leaving tomorrow. In the face of this irreversible transition, how do you choose from the mountain of accumulation what to take? Eventually you come upon a method, and in that suitcase (and maybe a carry-on) you place things that are useful, that bring you joy, that are beautiful.

I am settled into this elevated state and realize that I can now either play in the sea of impressions and visuals, or surface and work on my focus. It is obvious that I have done this countless times before. The eternal continuously pierces this plane, and the feeling is just blissful. This is always happening. A line from Rumi comes: "When you're inside the Kaaba it doesn't matter which direction you point your prayer carpet." I want to see the body of the Divine. The immediate answer: "What the hell do you think you're looking at? What more do you want?" Of course, what I want is for the Divine to conform to my projection and appear in recognizable human form.

Don Guillermo is singing something to the spirit manifestation to my right. 'She' is responding with laughter and unknown phonemes. My feeling is that she is stubborn and will not leave. Their interaction takes on a mythic bearing. This interplay is always happening, the shaman with the spirits. This has to happen. It is a living mythology that must be continuous for the world to be. I think of the Indian myth of Indra slaying the dragon Vṛtra in the *Ṛgveda*. It must be done over and over to release the waters. I hear Kal say, "(Incomprehensible name) is persistent in her presence tonight." Even though I feel intimately connected with all the proceedings, and that this mythic play is simultaneously a real event, for me, for everyone else, and for the cosmos, Kal's comment feels good in its verification.

There has been some more purging, some from the direction of where my wife Alethea sits. Even with a sliver of moonlight behind me I cannot see across the room. Absolute love for her just expands my heart. I know whatever she is going through it is all right. I look forward to the night ending and us cuddling.

I ask the question, "Who am I?" The answer is partly language and partly unveiling. "You are exactly who you are!" And I am shown. It is so obvious. I am this particular emanation from the Divine, and I exhibit these qualities in this combination. Neither Shiva nor Satan, this is all that being human is. The sense of self that generally thinks it runs things is now more or less an observational perspective.

Intermingled with the proceedings and musings, Don Guillermo brings us up individually and either sings or performs something specifically for our needs. He does a lot of reassuring laughing. Jan is sitting hugging her bucket, and he plays a pan flute melody that grabs deep within my bowels. He is drawing something out of her, and in resonance I feel something coming up within me. It is the closest to vomiting I get. "If you need to come out, come on." But she is the one convulsing in her bucket. Afterwards he blesses her by shaking some long bundled leaves in her face.

I am actually accustomed to this high state. I flit from insane geometric visuals to introspection. "What are my fears?" and they are laid as a banquet before me. In this place they are menu options. Fear of failure? Not hungry. A list of behavioral changes related to this fear scrolls down. Fear of mediocrity—now this is a tough one. I see it for example in my request of Alethea to never look at my writing until it is finished. I reverse the decision as a step towards ditching this monkey. This is all very easy to change, because there is no fear here. I realize that the real test is to do this after you come down, yet this feels like a true opportunity to pull the needle out of the stuck groove. Then I am gently berated for always playing it safe, delivered with infinite backing examples. Somehow my mind deems me cautious and conventional amidst blowing my reality apart with a powerful plant, a shaman voicing alien syllables, and vague spirits hovering while encircled by old and new friends regurgitating bad karma. Time to ask for another dose. I want to see snakes.

Waiting for a song to end, I sort of plop to my knees and crawl over and ask for more. Kal asks if I got high and I say "very much so" surprisingly like one who speaks English. Don Guillermo fills a glass, it goes down easily, but finding my chair in the dark causes a momentary quandary. There is one before me that appears empty so it must be my place. No place like home.

Kal gives a mythological tour of the planets. So…imagine you are on the moon. The moon is okay, but after a while you are dissatisfied there. The ground is sticky, movement is slow. So you go to Mercury. Here you have great ideas, you are filled with resolve and direction and knowing. But then you realize nothing is happening, just spinning your wheels…so…you go to Venus. Ah here is love, here is sensual delight. But after a while this is not quite satisfactory. All this sense indulgence leaves you wantonly irresolute, going nowhere…so…you go to Mars. Now you have order, you get things done. But soon this is also quite undesirable, you feel constrained, repeating the same things…so…you go to Jupiter. And here you are a benevolent ruler. You embody balance and good judgement in radiating all these qualities. Here's where our tour ends.

The second ayahuasca rush is not difficult to handle and I am in the same space, with the general intensity about doubled. There is a presence abiding behind or within the sparkly geometric fabric. I want to see but all I get are immense fluorescent lime-lightning outlines, humanoid, a little like the 'id-creature' in Forbidden Planet. They never quite coalesce, nor do they leave.

Back to my focus question. I ask it at three different junctures and the result does not alter. Now that I know who I am, ahem, what am I to do with this life? Answer: "There is absolutely nothing to do. You can eat a lot or not, read or not, work or not. You didn't come here with a specific purpose. It is all your choice." I am freed from my fate of having no fate. My choice, in this moment, is to radiate qualities of the divine that I swim in. Love is large, love is ridiculous, and my heart is bursting.

Don Guillermo is playing pan pipes for Sheryl, who is sitting in front of him. This song is a large snake coming up through me as me. Its head is as large as my chest, and that is where it stops. The next time I 'look', it is gone visually. I don't remember it disappearing, but the feeling of it within remains. I try to think about the particulars of a novel I am writing, but all I get is: "Don't be afraid to make it a celebration of your love."

Don Guillermo and Kal are speaking in Spanish and giggling hysterically like two drunken old men.

I wonder at the world I am privileged to reside in, at once mythic, geometric and eternal, and I wonder if it only exists through the plant's intervention and grace. Is it a closed system, or can it somehow converse with other living mythological pantheons, say Hindu or Greek? And what is it behind all these inbetween worlds that are given for humans to access and deal with the awful absolute unity of the ineffable? My mind depth seems a puddle with the ocean spread before me.

"Come amigo." Don Guillermo taps me and I get up and sit cross-legged before him. I notice that I am coming down. He blesses me, spraying aftershave, and sings a song of heartbreaking beauty. It is for me and I have no idea of its purpose. Let it speak to whatever I need. He brushes my face with a tied bundle of long leathery leaves, which feels exquisite. He tells me to fold my hands and does a cleansing ritual. I return in bliss.

Kal speaks about the Shipibo *curanderos*. They see life as the creation of great powerful beings. At their irresistible behest spirits are sent to incarnate here as the plants, animals and stones we see as our world. Normally the beings behind creation are so far removed that they are neither interested nor moved by human endeavor. However, through the spirits released by our destructive habit, word has gotten back to them that their creation is imperiled by us upstarts. They are not pleased, and earthquakes, drought, flood and the like are the result.

The songs work by luring the spirits with shimmering beauty, enticing them into the presence of the *curandero*. Once you have the attention of the spirit, information can be asked, whether for healing, knowledge or whatever. This is how you learn from the plants.

The last person Don Guillermo calls, Marla, adamantly refuses to go up. Talpo somehow realizes that she thinks Don Guillermo is offering her more ayahuasca. Last thing she needs. We all connect with her plight and laugh. "No mas. No mas!" comes from my throat. She goes and receives her song.

Now my connection with the previously unseen world is dissipating, and I look forward to exploring the horizontal realms with my love. The bullroarer sounds, and a thousand pterodactyls descend on the room. The spirit presence to my right has been gone for a while. Don Guillermo again gives thanks to the four directions, and Kal lights a candle, closing the circle. It is one in the morning. Four hours and several lifetimes have passed. People slowly get up and walk around, visit partners; some go to the bathroom to continue the great purge. Someone puts on a David Darling CD. Still pretty high, I make it across the room to Alethea, who apparently has had a rough night. She is still sick and too exhausted to move. She wants to lie down but is afraid of throwing up. She manages to convey that she had a vision of being in the cockpit with her father flying missions in WWII (he bombed Sicily and North Africa) and then began to purge, more for him than her.

I spend some time with her, participate in contrapuntal conversations, and eventually the coil unwinds and everyone has found a place to crash. Alethea has recovered her strength and is in good spirits. We chat and laugh and are asleep by three or four. As I go under I am granted one more vision. The ayahuasca vine grows straight up and then transforms into a huge oak tree. The branches continuously fan open, revealing a golden rainbow through the leaves.

We are up about 7:30, as is everyone else. Breakfast is a sonorous affair. We are new old friends, having passed this danger together. Most of us are giddy with the ingestion of butter and coffee and dairy for the first time in weeks. A box of jelly donuts disappears suspiciously quickly. We gather soon after on the main house's huge deck overlooking the lake. Everyone has a chance to relate as much or little of the evening as they wish.

Five of us in total purged. Kristen took three doses with zero effect. Marla, although mostly sick from both ends, did have several wonderful visions, especially Ganesh, the elephant-headed son of Shiva, upon whose back she flew. Suddenly there is a great horned owl on the shore of the lake, taking a bath, an activity no one has witnessed before. We feel blessed. Sandy, who sat and didn't drink the plant, had a vision of a great luminous snake in the room. Jack, who had a blissful experience his first time taking ayahuasca, was nearly catatonic and ill. Jan hugged her bucket all night, holding it for everyone. She had incredible visuals, being taken through various jungles and spirit worlds in preparation for her intensive two weeks with Don Guillermo in October. Talpo continued his journeying deep into the Pythagorean realms, where the golden cut of the phi ratio begins the elegant descent from the monad into the manifest. Sheryl had some visions and deep introspection. Sally, from whom I had heard the spirit manifest, apparently had a wondrous journey with only a vague recollection of sibilation. Catherine summed her night up: "Well, you buy your ticket, and you take your chance."

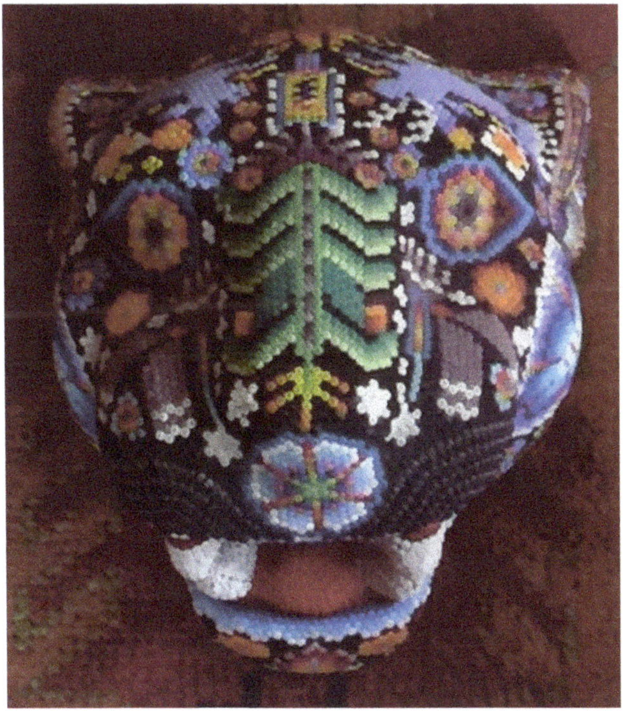

Beaded jaguar, Huichol artist, northern Mexico.

When asked, most voice that they would take ayahuasca again, even those who had been very ill. I feel that I would repeat the journey upon a calling of some sort, or if there is something I need to know or clear. We spend the rest of the day at Talpo and Sally's home in glorious lethargy. We drive back to Areopagus the next day, altered in unknown ways.

Postscript

Every evening for six days after the experience, at about one a.m., I find myself jolted into an aware and thought-free altered state for about two hours, echoing the ayahuasca high. I drift in and out of consciousness. One night, asleep on my right side, I awaken to a voice: "Turn over to your left side. We have work to do."

I am comfortable and don't want to move. The voice insists and I comply.

Mostly I dream of Don Guillermo and the spirit of ayahuasca. They are working with me in ways I little comprehend. It seems to end on the seventh day with an odd dream. I am in a nineteenth century sanitarium—opulent with fluted white columns and rangy lawns. Its clientele is exclusively comprised of composers with long white beards. I am privy to a consultation between Tchaikovsky and his psychiatrist. He is told that for therapy he can now only listen to one note, and a note is played on a lute. He asks if he can hear the same note over or just the one once. He is allowed the repetition.

The Sacred Origins of Western Civilization A Talk Given at Rudolf Steiner House Sydney, Australia 1 February 2011

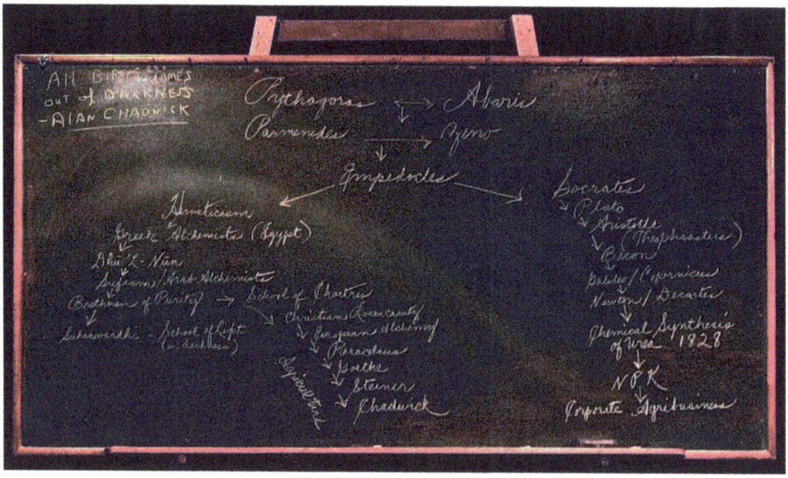

One story of western civilization.

I would like to start with one of my favorite things that Rudolph Steiner said: "It is the bird song that brings about the spring; bird song brings about the leaves opening up in the spring.[74]" I don't know if that has as much meaning for you all here in tropical Australia; I don't know if you exactly have a spring, but I assume that you have leaves that fall off and reemerge in some fashion. But I will leave that hanging with you, because behind all I'm going to discuss is the idea that this is a spiritual world that we live in. It is not a material world that we live in. And I think that is one of the ways that Rudolph Steiner saw this, something that very few people are able to see.

If you work in biodynamics and work with agriculture and work with the soil, you will find certain parts of yourself opening

74 Rudolf Steiner, *The Cycle of the Year as Breathing-Process of the Earth.*

up that otherwise wouldn't have. And you find that you feel the change of the seasons within your body. You realize that it is not some sort of physical, hard, solid world out there, but that it is actually a world within you. So I wanted to start there.

It is one of the core things that I picked up from Rudolph Steiner. I remember at one point last year in the fall, realizing that crickets are the ones that brought about the color change on the leaves. It was very clear. We happen to live in the mountains of North Carolina. That is one of the events that tourists drive from all over the country for, to come and drive two miles an hour to gawk at the leaves as they have become red and yellow. And it is worth it, because it is something special, and it happens every year. What goes unrealized is that seeing all that beautiful color on the mountains is a joy because it is experienced within, as your body. So this color change is the end, with the crickets, as it were, draining the green from the leaves, leaving the color, and the spring is the beginning with the birdsongs. Sound is a huge aspect of the movement of life.

And the other thing that is behind why I am here speaking is that this is kind of the leaf change of western civilization. I was very glad to see that someone is speaking here next week about WikiLeaks. It is really hard to see the political stuff from a spiritual perspective. I know that is something that Steiner worked with, and I was glad to see someone was working with that here.

So, western civilization—western culture—has basically lost its original story. Now with the native, original peoples—where I live the Native Americans: here, the Aboriginal people—they realize they have lost their original story. It is still a source of tears for them. And we—I will just speak for myself as a westerner, although obviously Australia is the West—we have lost not only our original story, but we have lost the memory of the fact that we had an original story, an original set of instructions, an original sacred origin. And the reality is that every civilization has come into being through some sort of revelation, some sort of coming about through the divine worlds.

Biodynamic gardener Alan Chadwick, tutored by Steiner as a teenager, said, "All birth comes out of darkness."

All seeds are encased in darkness. All birth, from everywhere, all the time, comes from darkness. So before I give you what I will tentatively call the forgotten myth of the origin of western civilization, I will give you, in a sort of thumbnail fashion, the widely accepted story that is handed down to us.

It is given out that in Greek times there were certain people who are now called pre-Socratic philosophers: people who lived and taught a few generations before the watershed event in western philosophy—the execution of Socrates by Athens. We are talking about Heraclitus, Empedocles, Parmenides, Thales, Pythagoras, and others. They lived around twenty-five hundred years ago. The standard idea is that the gods weren't quite what they used to be, they lost their grip on the Greek imagination, so these 'thinkers' started to explore the 'natural world'—'natural' is just as meaningless a term in philosophy as you would find on a package in the store. It just means it is from this planet somewhere. Pretty much every introduction to western philosophy will tell you that they sort of tinkered around in a proto-scientific way, trying to get a grasp on the physical world. So, in the centuries after they were gone, writers called them natural philosophers. And basically they reported that Empedocles came up with these four elements, Thales said the first cause is water, someone else said everything was made of fire. You know, they were kind of little children messing and guessing around. But eventually thinkers would grow up to be Aristotle, when they finally figured things out. But then when you really look at it, it turns out the people who were saying this about them were Aristotle and his followers. If you really read Aristotle, he bashes Pythagoras, and pretty much holds court over his predecessors. Plato does pretty much the same, but much more slyly than Aristotle.[75]

75 Of course, one of the reasons for this is that Aristotle's writings are mostly written out versions of his students' notes.

By the way, this is the oldest trick in the philosopher's handbook: "I'll tell you what so-and-so said, and then I'll critique it." I'm even doing it now.

So early on we have this idea that things are progressing. Parmenides supposedly invents logic—this is not the reality, we'll look at this in a minute—but by the time you get to Aristotle and Plato, logic is formalized into something opposite of what was intended. Then you go on this train to rationalism. Philosophically, what is rationalism? Rationalism bases itself on reason over experience. Thus rationalism is sort of an abstraction from lived life. Not only an abstraction, but it fosters the illusion that you can get to the real solely through thinking. Later on we'll see where that has taken us.

What I want you to understand here is this supposed story given us, that the West begins with these pre-Socratic infantile thinkers, who are supposedly improved upon and improved upon by better thinkers standing on their shoulders and seeing farther.

Now we are going right to what we're calling the sacred beginning of western civilization, around the sixth century B.C. What is right about this is based on the work of a mystic scholar named Peter Kingsley, and I'll take the blame for anything gone wrong. What Kingsley has done is re-looked at the pre-Socratics, and looked at the Greek language of these philosophers, looked at what they wrote meant at the time they wrote. Not what Aristotle said about them later. He really uncovered something. And because Peter Kingsley is a mystic, he is able to connect directly with what I'm going to call this tradition that founded western civilization.[76] It is really hard to talk about it. It doesn't have a name. I am not sure I even have the right to talk about it, but it desperately needs expression and recognition. It is very real and very subtle.

---

76 Much of what follows is based on Peter Kingsley's four books: *Ancient Philosophy, Mystery and Magic*; *In the Dark Places of Wisdom*; *Reality*; and *A Story Waiting to Pierce You*. Kingsley speaks more about this sacred tradition that founded western civilization in talks that are available at www.peterkingsley.org.

Kingsley's most recent book, *A Story Waiting to Pierce You*, partly concerns the encounter of Pythagoras with a very interesting shaman named Abaris the Hyperborean, about two-and-one-half thousand years ago. He performed a cleansing of Magna Graecia, which is the west coast of Anatolia, southern Italy, Sicily, and the mainland of Greece. This is the clearing of the ground for the planting of the seed of western culture.

And this seed carries within a mysterious relationship between Abaris, a shaman from Central Asia, Apollo, the god he carries within him, and Pythagoras, who is recognized as an incarnation of Hyperborean Apollo. And as you probably know, Apollo is not the god of rationalism, as Nietzsche said, but the god of cryptic oracles. Kingsley's book expresses the mystery of this meeting.

Parmenides (l) and Heraclitus (r), detail from "School of Athens" by Raphael, 1510-11.

The next significant founder of western civilization is Parmenides, and Parmenides wrote a poem. And in this poem he descends to the underworld. He is greeted by a goddess who is unnamed in the poem, but whom you can tell from the artifacts of the poem is Persephone—the goddess of the underworld. She not only gives him the gift of logic, but also gives him the gift of being as one. One, eternal, undivided, beginningless and endless. And logic initially, for Parmenides, as the goddess gave it to him, was a way to get back to oneness, a way to get from the confusing multiplicity of the world back into oneness. This is her gift to us that we have forgotten how to use. You can still see this in certain Buddhist logicians like Nagarjuna, for whom logic is actually used as a tool to cut through all illusory nature to get to the real.

Aristotelian logic—this is not my wheelhouse—states that there is A, and everything else is not-A. Or A is not B. In other words, logic serves to show separation, discreteness. Eastern logic is very different. They have what is called the 'four-cornered pillow of negation'. They agree that A is not B; also, A *is* B; then, neither A nor B; and then neither not A nor not B. Something like that. The point is that all these possibilities exist. For instance, my lovely wife Krys and I are not each other, yet on the soul level we are the same, sharing the same ground of being, and in another sense 'Krys' and 'Steve' are mere fictions and neither truly exist as entities.

I will try to give you another example from the Greek, as I understand things. Parmenides had a student, Xeno. You have heard of Xeno's paradoxes. Here's a quick demonstration: if I want to cross this room, I have to pass the halfway point. And then, once I reach this halfway point, I have to cross another halfway point. And so forth and so on. So, I can't cross the room. Once you get into Aristotle and his ilk in later ages, they don't understand that this is a logic that shows you the illusionary notion of distance, of separation. So this is how people like Xeno and Parmenides used logic to show that everything is one. Does that make any sense at all? It is a point that not too many people make, I think. Xeno and Parmenides are mystics, they are not devising little thought experiments to amuse themselves. True mysticism is practical, and we have lost this, and you, being Anthroposophists, are aware that Steiner's work was all about combining the spiritual and the practical.

We have to go deeper, literally. Parmenides gets his understanding not from his thinking, he gets it directly from the divine—from Persephone. He is literally getting it underground. In Greek it is called *katabasis*. He takes an underground journey. He is an initiate. With Pythagoras it's the same thing. He went underground. It is a particular practice called incubation. You would lie down in a temple precinct, or in a cave, in some very dark place. You would lie perfectly still—this stillness is called in Greek *hesychia*. It is a practice that was carried on into certain forms of Christian monasticism, especially in the Greek Orthodox Church and some of the Egyptian monasteries. So, Parmenides received, essentially, this blueprint for western civilization, from the goddess, in a revelation, from the underworld.

"Pythagoras Emerging from the Underworld" by Salvadore Rosa, 1662.

Parmenides received not only a revelation of the sacred nature of being: that being is one, unchanging, deathless, unmoving. He was also given specific knowledge about the illusory world. He was the first person who wrote about the earth being round; he also wrote about the tropics of Capricorn and Cancer. I don't think he called them that—he called them the tropics and the equator. He wrote about them from a little town off of the coast of southern Italy before anyone else did, a place called Velia. So he was given the structure of this world back then, lying in stillness, journeying deep within himself, and finding all of this within himself, revealed from a divine source.

Another of Parmenides' successors is Empedocles, living in Sicily. He comes up with the four elements, and is basically the father of all the sciences. And by the time Aristotle is looking back at him, and philosophers today looking back through the eyes of Aristotle, they are looking at him as playing with physical elements, the material world. But they are not physical for Empedocles. He is a mystic. He is a magician. They are the gods and goddesses: Earth is Hera, Fire is Hades, Air is Zeus. And while these are literally the building blocks of all the future western sciences: biology, chemistry etc., they all came out of this sacred soil. They had a sacred beginning that science has dismissed and forgotten.

Remember, Empedocles and all these mystics were essentially lying down, lying perfectly still, and then going deep, deep, deep within themselves into these dark places of wisdom. They were emerging with this structure of what was to be western civilization. They came out of these very dark places. But they came with instructions. If you read Empedocles, he says, before you do chemistry, there are certain ways that you have to breathe. There are certain attitudes that you have to have towards teachers, towards other people, things like that. There are ways of listening that must be mastered first. You can't just start using these teachings, and using them without recognizing their divine origin. Because they will eventually bite you from behind.

EMPEDOCLES PHILOSFUS.

P er ambition d'esser credulo unDio
Et gettosi nell'Etna d'nascosto,
Ma penso mal, che reseruano tosto
Le sue scarpe di ferro il suo deno

in Bassano per   753   *il Remondini*

Empedocles of Akragas. Line engraving by Remondini, 17th century.

Empedocles also wrote about a practice called common
sense. It is a way of holding all of your senses in common. It is a
really hard thing to think about feeling your feet on the floor at
the same time that you are hearing my voice, at the same time

that you are hearing the air conditioner, experiencing this heat. It is a really hard thing to do. Because you can't think your way through to it. But there is a way of going to the source of sensation, that is sort of a mystic state. At the heart of all sensation is this—again—is this oneness, which is a very dark place, but it is within ourselves. All of this is within ourselves. So eventually when you get to Aristotle, common sense—the experience of the ground of sensation—becomes desacralized. He says that everybody knows what common sense is, you know, every little kid has common sense. But originally it was this mystic practice. Do you have an idea now of what we have lost?

Temple of Hera in Akragas built during Empedocles' youth.

You see, I come from a country where, like in a Roadrunner cartoon, when someone runs off of a cliff, and they have that pregnant moment where they stop in mid-air, look down, and they realize that there is nothing underneath them. Well that is kind of where the United States is right now. It is a little scary, but it is also very interesting. The fact is, like anything organic—and all civilizations are organic—there is a germination, followed by a flourishment, and then it recedes back into the ground. And that's what is spurring me to talk about this. Some people are talking about it, but they talk about it in sort of very loose terms of the American empire ending. But I think it is something more than that. It is a certain perspective that was a twist of this original sacred origin that has to end. It has to.

I want to talk a little bit about how that happened. I was really surprised when I started looking into this, and I couldn't get around Plato. I was always a huge fan, you know—I have all his CD's—I just thought he was terrific. But if you read *The Republic*, and you read it closely, there are all sorts of troubling things. There is a program of eugenics. All art has to be in service of the state, or it is not allowed. There is rampant misogyny. There are a whole bunch of things that you either have to ignore or really look at and deal with. At a certain point you have to say, "Either this is some type of satire, or he really means this." And I don't know. But if you want to hold him as the paragon of western thinking, after which, as Whitehead famously said, everything else is a footnote, you have to do something to try and save Plato. And as it turns out, I couldn't.

Plato's two main allegories in *The Republic* are the allegory of the cave and the allegory of the line.[77] If you need a reminder, he is saying life is pretty much like living in a cave. You are chained, looking only straight ahead, and behind you is a fire. In front of the fire, but still behind you, people carry objects. So you look ahead, and see only the shadows of these objects projected in front of you. You think that is what reality really is: these shadows. And then someone can come and drag you kicking and screaming away, up to the light, to show you what is beyond the shadows. Makes sense, right?

But what totally amazed me—what he did—was he totally inverted the tradition that was handed to him. The tradition that was handed to him was that all light comes out of darkness.

77 Plato's cave allegory is found in Book 7 of his *Republic*, and the analogy of the line is in Book 6.

And that caves were the places where people went to obtain wisdom. They were also the places of initiation. You went to these dark places, incubated in stillness, and came in contact with the divinity. And Plato turned this whole method on its head, and said that now you have to leave the cave to get wisdom, since it's now the house of ignorance. And the stillness of incubation became this being chained in ignorance.

You could argue that this was necessary. That there was some evolutionary mandate necessary, we needed to take thought to its 'logical' conclusion. I don't know, I can only see what I see.

In some of Steiner's work I've read on Plato, he said that what Plato did was to exteriorize the mysteries in his dialogues. I'm not sure if Steiner thought it was a good thing or not, or maybe something was needed in the development of thinking. But basically it is true. Because the mysteries are always done underground, in temple precincts, in dark places, in caves. That is where wisdom is imparted. And the cave is the deepest part within yourself. So Plato in his inverted vision says, "No, no. It is out there somewhere. It is not within yourself." So where is it then? We need to look at the allegory of the line, which has four stages.

***REPUBLIC,* by Plato**
505e-511e
The Similies of the Sun and the Divided Line

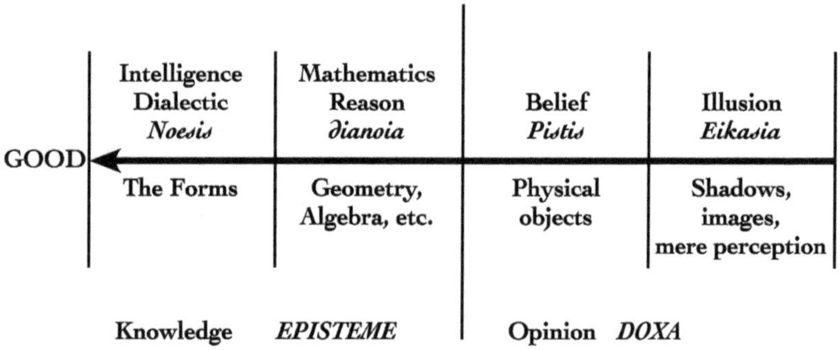

We'll try to keep this simple. The line is first divided in two, between knowledge and opinion. Those halves are both divided in two, for a total of four sections. The lowest stage is the senses. The second stage is belief based on the senses. The third stage is mathematics, and the highest stage is what Plato would call the good. And he never got around to saying quite what the good was, or the relationship between your life and the good, or objects and the forms they are based upon. He would just say there was some kind of participation. But you could never really pin him down on it. But basically what he does say is that the senses are worthless as a path to knowledge. And certainly many later Christian Gnostics take this to an extreme with their hatred of their own body and nature herself. But what is really real for Plato are abstract thoughts. Here are two quotes from *The Republic* about this:

> "...but what they really seek is to get sight of those realities which can only be seen by the mind."

> "...making no use whatsoever of any object of sense, but only of pure ideas moving on through to ideas ending with ideas."

Contrast that with the mystic tradition of Empedocles. He taught a practice of holding the senses in common, in stillness, to get to the unity, the oneness behind the senses. This is a huge shift, a complete reversal, promoted by Plato in his writings.

This is really the first stage of getting sucked out of your lived life, your sensation. Plato is saying, no, no, your lived senses are fooling you, but your thinking is what is really real. And all of western civilization since—all of it—has been different attempts to get to the real through thought. And it has never worked. And it is not going to. You can take physicists, they can go and have their string theories, and twenty-seven various dimensions, their little quantum anomalies, and they are not going to get there. Because they are looking out there somewhere.

If you take one thing home from this talk—hopefully it makes sense to you—is that the greatest fallacy of western philosophy, what took us off the tracks, is the idea that you can get to reality through thought.

That brings me to my favorite Einstein quote, that everyone must already know, "You can't solve a problem by using the same thinking that created the problem." I am paraphrasing. Politicians and especially environmentalists love to use it. Some different kind of thought will save the day. But Einstein did not go far enough, because the problem is thought itself. So, to sum up this point, the movement away from oneness into thinking, at least in philosophy, begins here with Plato. The ancient tradition that is the sacred origin of western civilization has to go elsewhere. It didn't end there, though, as we shall try to show later, and this stream went underground.

Before that, I am going to take you happily skipping to where this shift into thinking led. What happens with Aristotle is that logic becomes kind of codified. What becomes important, what becomes real, are the classifications of things. He puts his stake in various kinds of classifications and delineations of things. The Romans, of course, were *really* practical, without the messy mysticism. I can say that because my grandparents were born in Sicily, right near Empedocles' home town. To take a great short cut, classical learning is lost in Europe after the fall of Rome, and is reintroduced through the Muslim world. Thomas Aquinas is huge in the reintroduction of Aristotle through Arabic translations in Andalusia. Simplifying, there is a split with him, between faith for all things pertaining to God, and Aristotelian rationalism for all things pertaining to science.

I want to show you now how this abstraction from living life got worse and worse in the West. You have then someone like Francis Bacon in England—is there anyone here who thinks Bacon wrote Shakespeare? You have Bacon, who brings in the idea that knowledge is power. And what knowledge is, is power over nature. So that the only use for knowledge is not to become the real, but to have power and control over things and people and nature.

The next huge abstraction takes place with Copernicus and Galileo, where we moved from a geocentric worldview to a heliocentric worldview. And the Greeks were aware of this, at least some of the Greeks knew, and it was written about, that the earth went around the sun. But that is not how life is lived. What happens at this point is huge: your senses are wrong. You wake up, you watch the sun move across the sky like this, but you are told it is not real. What really happens is this other movement of earth around the sun that you have to think about. According to Aristotle, one or the other must be true. But from the mystic point of view, both are real. Another point about Galileo—both he and Pythagoras said that the universe, the cosmos, consists of number. The difference between them is that for Galileo number is quantity, and for Pythagoras number is quality.

So again, what is real is a thought about things, and not what you are living. That is huge; you can see the quick declination after this. You go from Newton where you have the further abstraction of the world as a clockwork machine; you have Descartes, who really just slices things off with his *I think therefore I am*. Now we have being predicated on thought, instead of the other way around. "I am because I think I am"? See how far we have completely severed ourselves from what I am calling the tenets of this primordial tradition. We began with being as oneness, and now have buried being under thought.

And then, because we are practitioners of biodynamics, this is how it applies there. Of course, biodynamics comes about, you probably know, because Ehrenfried Pfeiffer asked Steiner, "Why aren't your teachings sticking? You are giving all these great teachings, you have this great presence, and they're not sticking?" Steiner said, "It is the food. The cosmic is no longer in the food. And therefore, it is not in us. It has nothing to grab hold of inside us."

Even going back to 1828, when there were a number of people, Goethe being among them, in this physicalist vs. vitalist controversy. The crowning achievement of the physicalists was to synthesize an organic product, which was urea. That happened in 1828 in Germany. And that led to plastics and what have you. And it led to this whole farming through NPK—synthetic nitrogen, potassium and phosphorus—and it was already underway in Steiner's time. The whole declination of everything went on in his lifetime.

Eventually you have Monsanto and—this came out on WikiLeaks—the United States was going to punish any European country that did not take Monsanto's seeds. Spain and France were mainly the ones who were targeted, using military language, war metaphors. This is sick. This is a dying animal. I know this is not happy news, I am sorry.

Ok, I'll give you my Obama take now. And this came to me, from the spiritual point of view—and the spiritual and the practical are really the same—that in order to get past where we are at—because there is no tweaking it, there is no fixing it—it requires a certain amount of giving up. In other words, giving up on trying to fix it. The whole thing about Obama—and I got caught up in it too, not so long ago—but for those of us who lived through the Bush years, that was horrific. So Obama has this whole thing about hope. The *Audacity of Hope* is the name of his book, and there's all this about hope, hope, hope. I realized that from the spiritual level, his job actually is to end hope. Because if you had any hope in him, where is your hope now? It is over.

You get the idea. On a spiritual level, his job, though he obviously doesn't know it, is to bring us to this point of hopelessness. At least it worked for me. There is nothing redeemable in the current corporate system, there is no salvation from these guys. It has to just finish.

But I wanted to tie in—some of this is fairly speculative—the movement of this tradition, where it goes after Greece, because maybe there is a tie-in with Steiner. It really kind of bailed out of Athens. It moved into Greek hermeticism and into the hermetic tradition in Egypt, also known as the Greek alchemists. There were already many Greek colonies in Egypt. Peter Kingsley traces the tradition into Islamic Egypt, the alchemists and early Sufis there. There are many instances of Empedocles being seen as a living teacher for these people. To claim someone outside of Islam as your teacher meant you were serious.

"Preparing Medicine from Honey" 'Abdullah ibn al-Fadl from an Arabic translation of the Materia Medica of Dioscorides, Iraq, 1224.

For example there is Dhu'l Nun, who is kind of the father of the Sufis—many of the Sufi lineages trace themselves back to him in ninth century Egypt. He is one of these alchemists. You can see it with the Ismailis, who were combining Hermetic Greek and Islamic ideas. And the Ismailis seem to be connected with the Ikwan al-Safa. The Ikwan al-Safa—which translates to 'The Brethren of Purity'—were a monastic group within Islam who used Pythagorean number theory in describing the world and the body. Very interesting group, who were centered in Basra and other places in what is now Iraq, in areas currently being devastated.

The speculation, or suspicion I've always had, is that this is the group that Christian Rosencrantz encountered when he went East looking for wisdom. Steiner writes about this: the story, I believe, is that he goes to Damascus and brings back some kind of wisdom that goes into Rosicrucianism, and eventually Anthroposophy. And this is the time period when the Brethren of Purity are flourishing. They appear to be the most likely candidates, and I always like to think that there are more connections than separations between esoteric Islam and the West.

And then you have Suhrawardi, who was martyred in the 1100's for combining Islam with earlier Persian traditions. He founded the School of Light, but again, in his writings, this light is coming out of the darkness. Darkness is the source of the light. Suhrawardi writes about Empedocles being one of his teachers, part of his lineage. So it's amazing that there is this whole tradition running through Islam about Empedocles being a living teacher for them, 1500 years after his death.

I've also had a suspicion that some aspect of this sacred tradition came back through Islam to the West to inform the School of Chartres. I don't know if any of you have ever been to Chartres Cathedral—to me it is the peak of western architecture. It is an amazing place. It is so structured that the goddess still lives there. And the goddess for them is called Natura. It's the only time I can think of in Christianity that nature is revered as a goddess. There are no crosses in the cathedral, no burials; the cathedral is completely dedicated to life.

Persian miniature of a Sufi meditating in the trunk of a çinar tree, 1500's.

The interesting thing is that there are 1500 statues in Chartres, and not one of Plato. There is a statue of everyone—but there is no Plato there. He is conspicuous by his absence. To Platonists, especially. Pythagoras has multiple representations. It feels to me that it is a Pythagorean masterpiece. Of course, not to throw the baby out with the bathwater, so much of Pythagorean thought is transmitted through Plato, especially in his *Timaeus*. But it was just amazing what happened in France at that time, and it was all anonymous. Nobody knows who built Chartres, nobody signed anything, nobody knows how it was built, or anything. It was not that long ago, in certain ways.

Anyway, because I was coming here to Rudolf Steiner House, I was trying to trace that maybe some part of this tradition found its way and wove through Christian Rosencrantz, to Paraselsus, who was a plant alchemist, and then through Goethe and then to Steiner. And then into biodynamics.

So to tie this up personally, Krys and I have a biodynamic farm in the mountains of North Carolina, and a friend of ours studied under Alan Chadwick, who I believe is as great a mystic of the garden as there ever was. Alan Chadwick studied as a teenager under Steiner. Steiner tutored him while he was in England. Alan Chadwick, who died in 1980, also went to Switzerland to study with Steiner. Alan Chadwick didn't write anything, but he gave talks. We have an archive of over two hundred of his talks, and established our own publishing company to get them out. The book is called *Performance in the Garden*. In the United States, mostly in California, Alan Chadwick had hundreds of students. And basically he really got the ball rolling on one level, and is as responsible for the success of biodynamics in America as anyone. He wasn't as much of a purist as, say, Pfeiffer. Or a scientist. He said, "I'm not a student of Steiner's, but a child of Steiner's." He was more akin to Parmenides or Empedocles, trying to point the students in his gardens the way to unity with nature, the greatest teacher. He always talks about getting out of what he called 'the thought-box', away from thinking, into direct connection.

On our farm we do the preps and follow basic biodynamic protocol. I will say this about biodynamics: on our farm, last year there was record heat, the year before that was record rainfall. The two years before that was record drought. We managed—the elementals were kind to us, or were reciprocally kind to each other—we were able to get something going in those years. Even after two years of drought, our two springs had no water, at all, for half of the year. Yet we produced some beautiful food. So I know biodynamics works. I don't really understand what Steiner says about nitrogen, or his particular take on chemistry, but I know biodynamics works.

This is why certain things like biodynamics are so important. And it connects back to what I said earlier about Empedocles and the four elements. For him they are divine, not material. And this has to be our approach to every aspect of life.

So we've done some kind of circle here. Biodynamics is something Steiner did at the end of his life. To me, I think, it was the thing that he did that was most important; it has the most impact at this time, needed today more than ever. That direct connection with nature, with life, may be the only thing to carry into the future.

This primordial tradition I've been talking about, it has no name, it kind of just weaves in and out and helps other sacred traditions at times. But it also seems to be a tradition that shows up at the beginning and at the end, guiding the creation and dissolution of civilizations. And it seems we are at the end now.

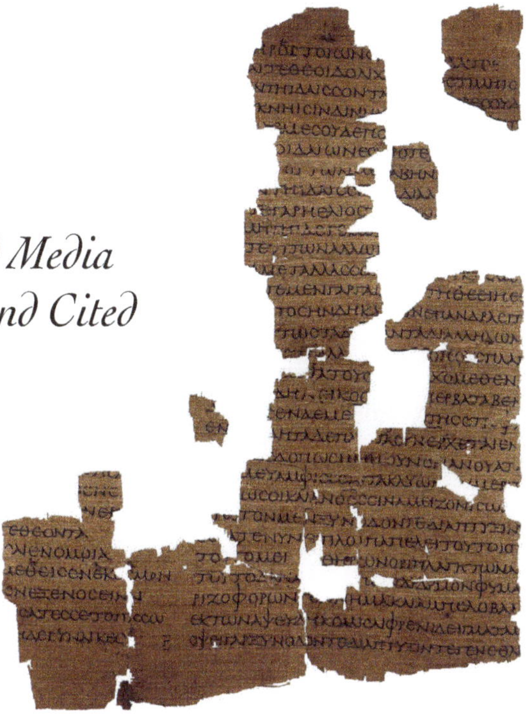

Texts and Media Consulted and Cited

Adair, Robert K. *The Physics of Baseball: Third Edition, Revised, Updated and Expanded*. New York: Harper Collins Perennial, 2002.

Affatigato, Tom. "Foundations of Yogic Culture: Vedic Methodology and McClain's Musicology." *Moksha Journal,* Vol. 2, No. 1, 1985.

Al-Alwan, Muna. "Reading Shakespeare Cross-Culturally: An Islamic Approach." *Sacred Web,* #30, January 2013.

Bamford, Christopher, editor, *Homage to Pythagoras: Rediscovering Sacred Science*. Hudson, NY: Lindisfarne Press, 1994.

Barber, C. L. "Magical and Mundane Shakespeare." *The New York Review of Books,* 16 October, 1975.

Beckwith, Christopher I. *Greek Buddha: Pyrrho's Encounter with Early Buddhism in Central Asia*. Princeton University Press, 2015.

Blackhirst, Rodney. *Primordial Alchemy and Religion: Essays on Traditional Cosmology*. San Rafael, CA: Sophia Perennis, 2008.

Bolton, J. D. P. *Aristeas of Proconnesus*. Oxford University Press, 1962.

Bormann, Edwin. *The Shakespeare-Secret*. London: T. Wohlleben, 1895.

Brown, Robert K., and Comfort, Philip W., trans. *The New Greek Interlinear Testament*. Wheaton, IL: Tyndale House, 1990.

Burkert, Walter. *Lore and Science in Ancient Pythagoreanism*. Harvard University Press, 1972.

Burns, Theresa. "Frances Garland, William Shakespeare, and John Dees' Green Language." *Journal of the Western Mystery Tradition*, No. 15, Vol. 2, Autumnal Equinox, 2008.

Cadwalla, Carole. "Are the robots about to rise? Google's new director of engineering thinks so…" *The Guardian*, 22 February 2014.

Calasso, Roberto. *Ardor*. New York: Farrar Straus and Giroux, 2014.

Carrière, Jean-Claude. *The Mahabharata*, Peter Brook, trans. New York: Harper and Row, 1985.

Caruso, Carl. "Sacred Pearls in the Machinery of Hamlet." *The Oxfordian*, Vol. X, 2007.

Chadwick, Alan. *Performance in the Garden*. Asheville, NC: Logosophia, LLC, 2008.
—*Reverence, Obedience and the Invisible in the Garden*. Asheville, NC: Logosophia, LLC, 2013.

Chapple, Christopher, and Kelly, Eugene P. *The Yoga Sūtras of Patañjali: An Analysis of the Sanskrit with Accompanying English Translation*. Delhi: Sri Satguru Publications, 1990.

Coburn, Thomas B. *Encountering the Goddess: A Translation of the Devī-Māhātmya and a Study of its Interpretation*. State University of New York Press, 1991.

de Nicholás, Antonio. *Avatara: The Humanization of Philosophy Through the Bhagavad Gita.* New York: Nicholas Hays, Ltd., 1976.
—*Four-Dimensional Man: Meditations Through the Ṛg Veda*. New York: Nicholas Hays Ltd., 1976.

Doniger, Wendy, trans. *The Rig Veda: An Anthology*. New York: Penguin Books, 1981.

Dodds, E. R. *The Greeks and the Irrational.* University of California Press, 1951.

Dyczkowski, Mark S. G. *The Doctrine of Vibration: An Analysis of the Doctirnes and Practices of Kashmir Shaivism*. State University of New York Press, 1987.

Eckersley, Sylvia. *Number and Geometry in Shakespeare's* Macbeth*: The Flower and the Serpent*. Edinburgh: Floris Books, 2007.

Eliade, Mircea, *The Myth of the Eternal Return: Or, Cosmos and History*. Princeton University Press, 1954.

Eliot, T.S. "Hamlet and His Problems." *The Sacred Wood*, 1921.

Fideler, David. *Jesus Christ, Sun of God: Ancient Cosmology and Early Christian Symbolism*. Wheaton, IL: Quest Books, 1993.

Figueira, Dorothy. *The Hermeneutics of Suspicion: Cross-Cultural Encounters with India*. London: Bloomsbury Academic, 2015.

Frank, Adam. "Dreaming in Code: Michio Kaku's 'Future of the Mind.'" *New York Times Book Review*, March 7, 2014.

Gemelli Marciano, M. Laura. "Images and Experience: At the Root of Parmenides' *Aletheia*." *Ancient Philosophy*, 28, 2008.

Geuter, Marie. *Herbs in Nutrition*. Bio-Dynamic Agricultural Association, 1978.

Goldman, Peter. "Hamlet's Ghost: A Review Article." *Anthropoetics*, 7, No. 1, Spring/Summer 2001.

Greenblatt, Stephen. *Hamlet in Purgatory*. Princeton University Press, 2001.

Griffith, Ralph T. H., *Hinduism: The Rig Veda*. New York: Book-of-the-Month Club, 1992.

Hamilton, Edith, and Cairns, Huntington, Eds. *The Collected Dialogues of Plato*. Princeton University Press, 1961.

Hopkins, Thomas J. *The Hindu Religious Tradition*. Belmont, CA: Wadsworth Publishing Company, 1971.

Hunter, Robert. *A Box of Rain: Collected Lyrics*. New York: Viking, 1990.

James, E. O. *The Cult of the Mother Goddess*. New York: Barnes and Noble Books, 1994.

Jorgensen, Paul A. "A Formative Shakespearian Legacy: Elizabethan Views of God, Fortune, and War." *PLMA*, Vol. 90, No. 2, Mar. 1975.

Kingsley, Maria, and Kingsley, Peter. "As Far as Longing Can Reach." *Parabola*, Summer 2006.

Kingsley, Peter. *Ancient Philosophy, Mystery and Magic*. Oxford University Press, 1997.

—*In the Dark Places of Wisdom*, 1999, Inverness, CA: The Golden Sufi Center.

—*Reality*. Inverness, California: The Golden Sufi Center, 2003.

—*Everything: The Record of an Extraordinary Event*. CD 4 "Incubation." Recorded at the Abode, New Lebanon, NY, October 2006.

—Radio interview with Gary Null, 5 August 2008.

—*A Story Waiting to Pierce You: Mongolia, Tibet and the Destiny of the Western World*. Inverness, CA: The Golden Sufi Center, 2010.
—"Original Instructions: An Interview with Peter Kinksley." *Quest*, Summer 2011. Interview with Richard Smoley.
—*The Elders*, CD released 2015. In 2010, at Cavallo Point in California, Peter Kingsley was invited to address the theme of sacred origins in a joint session with Chief Oren Lyons, Faithkeeper for the Onondaga Nation of the Iroquois Confederacy.

Lawlor, Robert, *Sacred Geometry: Philosophy and Practice*. New York, Crossroad Publishing, 1982.

Lee, Mark Owen. *The Myth of Orpheus and Eurydice in Western Literature*. Ph.D. thesis, The University of British Columbia, 1960.

Lengyel, Emil. *1000 Years of Hungary: A Short History*. New York: John Day Co. 1958.

Lings, Martin. "Hamlet." Temenos Academy Lecture. 1993.
—*Shakespeare's Window into the Soul: The Mystical Wisdom in Shakespeare's Characters*. Rochester, Vermont: Inner Traditions, 2006.

Mannikka, Eleanor. *Angkor Wat: Time, Space, and Kingship*. University of Hawaii Press, 1996.

McLain, Ernest. *The Pythagorean Plato: Prelude to the Song Itself*. Stony Brook, NY: Nicolas Hays, LTD, 1978.
—*The Myth of Invariance: The Origin of the Gods, Mathematics and Music from the Ṛg Veda to Plato*. York Beach, ME: Nicolas-Hays, Inc., 1984.

Meyer, Martin W., Ed. *The Ancient Mysteries: Sacred Texts of the Mystery Religions of the Ancient Mediterranean World*. New York: Harper and Row, Publishers, 1987.

Michell, John. *Dimensions of Paradise*. New York: Harper and Row, 1988.
—*Who Wrote Shakespeare?* London: Thames and Hudson, 1996.

Michell, John, and Rhone, Christine. *Twelve Tribe Nations and the Science of Enchanting the Landscape*. London: Thames and Hudson, 1991.

Milne, Joseph. "Hamlet: The Conflict between Fate and Grace." Temenos Academy Lecture, 1992. Audio cassette.

—"Hamlet: The Conflict Between Fate and Grace." *Hamlet Studies*, 18.1-2, Summer-Winter 1996. (Slightly revised transcription of the above lecture.)

—"The Eternal Drama: A Study of Shakespeare's Cosmic Vision." Temenos Academy Lecture, 1998. Audio cassette.

—*The Ground of Being: Foundations of Christian Mysticism*, London: The Temenos Academy, 2004.

Milward, Peter. *Biblical Influences in Shakespeare's Tragedies*. Indiana University Press, 1987.

Minnema, Lourens. *Tragic Views of the Human Condition: Cross Cultural Comparisons between Views of Human Nature in Greek and Shakespearean Tragedy and the Mahābhārata and Bhagavadgītā*. New York and London: Bloomsbury, 2013.

Nasr, Seyyed Hossein. *Knowledge and the Sacred.* New York: Crossroad, 1981.

—"Echoes of Infinity: An Interview with Seyyed Hosein Nasr." *Parabola*, Spring 1988.

Ortega Y Gasset, Jose. *Meditations on Quixote*. New York: W.W. Norton and Co., 1963.

—*Historical Reason*. New York: W.W. Norton, 1984.

Pollack, Rachel. *The Body of the Goddess: Sacred Wisdom in Myth, Landscape and Culture*. Rockport, MA: Element Books, 1997.

Prechtel, Martín. *The Unlikely Peace at Cuchumaquic: The Parallel Lives of People as Plants: Keeping the Seeds Alive.* Berkeley, CA: North Atlantic Books, 2012.

Poole, Adrian. *Tragedy: Shakespeare and the Greek Example*. London: Basil Blackwell Ltd, 1987.

Radakrishnan, S., *The Principal Upaniṣads*. New York: Harper and Brothers, 1953.

Ram, Alur Janaki. "Arjuna and Hamlet: Two Moral Dilemmas." *Philosophy East and West,* 18 (1/2), 1968.

Salaman, Clement, van Oyen, Dorine, Wharton, William D., and Mahé, Jean-Pierre, trans. *The Way of Hermes: New Translations of* The Corpus Hermeticum *and* The Definitions of Hermes Trismegistus to Asclepius. Rochester, VT: Inner Traditions, 2004.

Sargeant, Winthrop, trans. *The Bhagavad Gita*. The State University of New York Press, 1984.

Schimmel, Annemarie. *Mystical Dimensions of Islam*. University of NC Press, 1975.
—*The Mystery of Numbers*. Oxford Press, 1993.

Schneider, Michael, *A Beginner's Guide to Constructing the Universe: The Mathematical Archetypes of Nature, Art, and Science*. New York, Harper Collins, 1994.

Shakespeare, William. *The Tragical History of Hamlet, Prince of Denmark*. Cyrus Hoy, ed. New York: W.W. Norton and Company, 1993.

Shapero, Hannah M.G., "The Diamond Way: Baseball as Esoteric Ritual." *Gnosis: A Journal of the Western Inner Traditions*, No. 11, Spring 1989.

Shiva, Vandana. "The Food Dharma", *The Asian Age,* 10 September, 2015.

Smith, Christine Bustato. "Ophelia and the Perils of the Sacred Feminine." *Multicultural Shakespeare: Translation, Appropriation and Performance*, Vol. 6/7, 2010.

Sohmer, Steve. "Certain Speculations on *Hamlet,* the Calendar, and Martin Luther." *Early Modern Literary Studies*, 2.1, 1996.

Solomon, Jon, Ed. *Apollo: Origins and Influences*. The University of Arizona Press, 1994.

Steiner, Rudolf. *The Cycle of the Year as Breathing-Process of the Earth: The Four Great Festival-Seasons of the Year*. Anthroposophic Press, 1984.

Stewart, Doug, "The Old Ball Game." *Smithsonian,* Vol. 29 No. 7, October 1998.

Strachan, Gordon. *Chartres: Sacred Geometry, Sacred Space*. Edinburgh: Floris Books, 2003.

Ustinova, Yulia. *Caves and the Ancient Greek Mind: Descending Underground in the Search for Ultimate Truth*. Oxford University Press, 2009.

Uždavinys, Algis, ed. *The Golden Chain: An Anthology of Pythagorean and Platonic Philosophy*. Bloomington, IN: World Wisdom, Inc., 2004.

Warner, Rosemary. *Shakespeare's Ark*. Stonecrop Publishing, 2008.

Waterfield, Robin. *The Theology of Arithmetic: On the Mystical, Mathematical and Cosmological Symbolism of the First Ten Numbers; Attributed to Iamblichus*. Grand Rapids, MI: Phanes Press, 1988.

West, M. L. *The Orphic Poems*. Oxford: Clarendon Press, 1998.

Wheelwright, Philip, ed. *The Presocratics*. New York: Macmillan Publishing Company, 1966.

Wilson, Peter Lamborn. *Ploughing the Clouds: The Search for Irish Soma*. San Francisco: City Lights Books, 1999.

Yates, Frances A. *The Art of Memory*. University of Chicago Press, 1966.
—*Shakespeare's Last Plays: A New Approach*. New York: Routledge and Keegan Paul, 1975.

Zimmerman, Ira B. director. *Shakespeare's Spirituality: A Perspective: An Interview with Dr. Martin Lings*. DVD, 2006.

Photo and Illustration Credits

All illustrations are public domain except where noted.

3 Evelyn De Morgan, "Lux in Tenebris", 1895.

7 Yantra painting 1700's, Museo Nacional de Anthropologia, Madrid.

12 Hermes, Eurydice and Orpheus, fifth century BC, National Archeological Museum of Naples.

14 Gaetano Gandolfi, "Orpheus and Eurydice", 1700's, Private collection.

16 Gustav Moreau, "Thracian Girl Carrying the Head of Orpheus on His Lyre", 1865. Musée d'Orsay, Paris.

24 Indra, 1300's, Patan Museum, Nepal.

27 Saraswati, 1100's, Gujarat.

38 Yama, Mongolia 1700's, Jacques Marchais Museum, New York City.

51 Arjuna Sculpture, Bali.

51 John Barrymore as Hamlet, 1922, photo by Francis Bergman.

55 Ettore Ferrari, "Trial of Giordano Bruno", bronze relief, 1800's.

57 Henri Gillard Glindoni, "John Dee Performing an Experiment before Queen Elizabeth", late 1800's, Wellcome Library.

62 Pedro Américo, "Visão de Hamlet", 1890, Pinacoteca do Estado de São Paulo.

68 John William Waterhouse, "Ophelia", 1910, private collection.

92 Kṛṣṇa and Arjuna, folio from the 1800's.

94 Kṛṣṇa appears to Arjuna as Viṣṇu Vishvarupa, Indian miniature, 1700's.

107 Hungarian actress Török Irma as Ophelia in 1901.

113 Alexandre Cabanel, "Ophelia", 1883, private collection.

118 Indian map of the *nadis*.

127 Orpheus mosaic, 194 BC, recently returned to Turkey by the Dallas Museum after they learned it was stolen from Şanlıurfa in1998.

132 Orpheus on his lyre, North Africa, 200's.

136 Adam Elsheimer, "The Stoning of Saint Stephen", 1604, Scottish National Gallery.

138 North Rose Window, Chartres Cathedral.

139 Gustave Dore, "Beatrice leads Dante through the Ninth Heaven", 1868.

143 Evelyn De Morgan, "Luna", 1885.

147 Alexandre Auguste Hirsch, "Calliope Teaching Orpheus", 1865.

152 The various enclosures of Angkor Wat represent each of the Yugas.

160 All figures drawn by Susan Yost.

162 Hannah M.G. Shapero, "The Diamond Way: Baseball as an Esoteric Ritual". Thanks to Pyracantha for permission to use her graphic. Her website is www.pyracantha.com.

164 Chartres Cathedral, West Portal, photo by Krys Crimi.

169 Parmenides statue in the Velia Archeological Park, Italy. © REDA & CO

181 Beaded jaguar, contemporary Huichol artist, northern Mexico, photo by Krys Crimi.

183 Backdrop to Sydney Talk, putative lineages, photo by Krys Crimi

187 Raphael, "The School of Athens", Parmenides and Heraclitus detail, 1510-11, Vatican Museum.

189 Salvadore Rosa, "Pythagoras Emerging from the Underworld", 1662, Kimbell Art Museum.

191 Remondini, line engraving of Empedocles, 1600's.

192 Temple of Hera, Agrigento, Italy, © José Luiz Bernardes Ribeiro

199 'Abdullah ibn al-Fadl, "Preparing Medicine from Honey", from an Arabic translation of the *Materia Medica* of Dioscorides, Iraq, 1224, Metropolitan Museum of Art.

201 Persian miniature, Sufi meditating in the trunk of a çinar tree, 1500's, Reza Abassi Museum, Teheran.

205 Strasbourg Papyrus of Empedocles, late first century AD.

221 Bio photo taken at the Temple of Apollo at Didyma spring 2015 by Krys Crimi.

Acknowledgements

Beggar that I am, I am even poor in thanks; but I thank you…
– Hamlet

If I have one trait even fractionally in common with the incomparable Socrates, it is in knowing what I do not know. He had his mysterious Diotima to tutor him, and I have been in Fortuna's bosom enough to encounter and work with people of great depth and quality—within and without traditional academia—from whom I have taken more than given, especially in the realms of learning how to think, and, inseparably, of learning how and when not to think. Recognizing them in vaguely chronological order, my parents: Frances and Angelo, Brenda Wineapple, Gurani Añjali, Eugene Kelly, Dorothy Figueira, Keith Critchlow, and Peter and Maria Kingsley.

Thanks to *Katabatic Wind*'s, intrepid readers, enduring early draftiness and offering instrumental suggestions: Eric Friedwald, Mindi Meltz and Jeff Baker. Especially Mindi, whose close reading precipitated the thorough rewrite the the book needed and deserved. Thanks also to Susan Yost, whose design talents leave me gratefully awestruck. And eminently and lovingly, my first and continuous sounding-board and springboard for all this manuscription, my partner and playmate for three decades, Krys.

Thanks to Betty Roznak for permission to use "Details of a Second Occultation" as the epigraph. Her poetry has the force and timbre of revelation. Thanks to David Sylvian for generous permission to use the lyrics of his song "Orpheus." He has been composing beautifully profound music since the 80's. Thanks to Robert Hunter for permission to print the lyrics to "Saint Stephen," which I heard—and synesthetically *saw*—at my first Grateful Dead show in 1977, and never again. And thanks to all the known and unknown artists whose work illustrates this text, adding a dimension of sublimity words can only reach for.

Lastly, writing for me becomes more enjoyable under the influence of ambient music, so I would like to thank the following composers and bands for their work in generating homeopathic sonic antidotes to the adrenal-jarring clangor anyone bearing witness to our days must too-often endure. Brian Eno, the aforementioned David Sylvian, Harold Budd, Alessandra Celletti, Alio Die, Marconi Union, Robert Fripp, Robin Guthrie, Vassilis Tsabropoulos, Bill Laswell, Michael Brook, Chad Lawson, Rachel Grimes, Kudsi Erguner, Six Organs of Admittance, Derya Turkan, Hammock, Hossein Alizadeh, Loscil, Lunz, Munir Bachir, Laurence Ball, Itsyounotme, Kayhan Kalyor, Bvdub, Labradford, 0, Jordan De La Serra, Grouper, Eberhard Weber, Anouar Brahem, Meg Bowles, John Foxx, G.I. Gurdjieff and Thomas de Hartmann come to mind and deserve all our thanks.

Biography

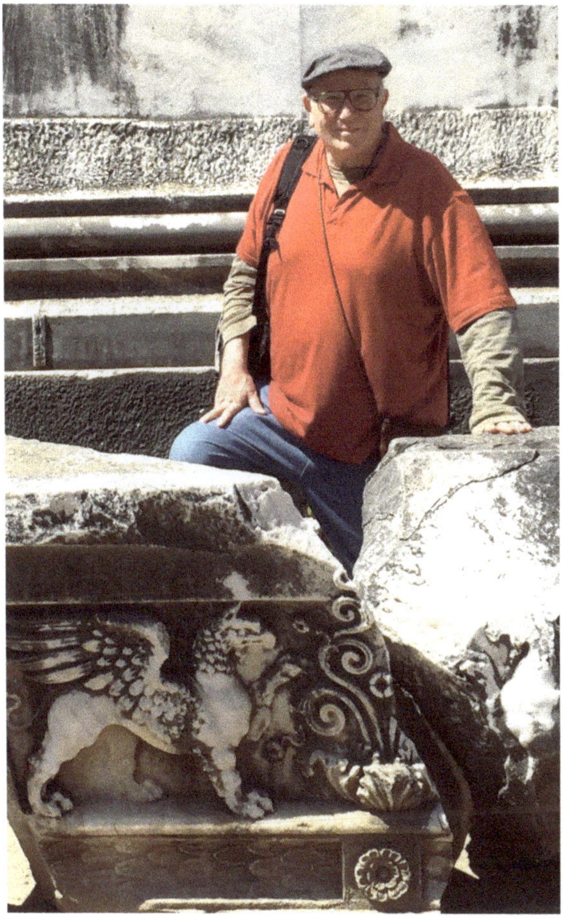

Stephen Crimi has a degree in English literature from Union College, and spent over a decade in traditional Yoga study at Yoga Anand Ashram in Amityville, NY. He's done time as an editor, estate gardener, cook, massage therapist, and most recently, running a biodynamic garden and fiber farm, Philosophy Farm, for twelve years with his wife of three decades, Krys. They now live in the city of Asheville where they continue to garden. Stephen was born in Brooklyn, and raised on the streets of Ozone Park, NYC.

www.ingramcontent.com/pod-product-compliance
Lightning Source LLC
Chambersburg PA
CBHW040412110426
42812CB00033B/3356/J
9780996639415